the threefold refuge in the theravāda buddhist tradition

the threefold refuge in the theravāda buddhist tradition

edited by
john ross carter
with
george doherty bond
edmund f. perry
shanta ratnayaka

anima books 1982

Cover illustration is the Buddha image in the Washington Buddhist Vihara Shrine Room, created at the Vihara by Sri Lankan sculptor Prabhath Wijesekara. It has been furnished through the courtesy of the Vihara.

Library of Congress Cataloging in Publication Data
Main entry under title:
The Threefold refuge in the Theravada Buddhist tradition.
Bibliography: p.
Includes index.
Contents: "The notion of 'refuge' (sarana) in the Theravada Buddhist tradition" / by John Ross Carter — "The Buddha as refuge in the Theravada Buddhist tradition" / by George D. Bond. — "Dhamma as refuge in the Theravada Buddhist tradition" / by John Ross Carter — [etc.]
1. Threefold refuge—Addresses, essays, lectures.
2. Theravada Buddhism—Addresses, essays, lectures.
I. Carter, John Ross.

BQ4350.T47 1982 294.3'42 82-16467
ISBN 0-89012-030-7

Printed in USA

ANIMA BOOKS is a subdivision of Conococheague Associates, Inc., 1053 Wilson Avenue, Chambersburg, Pennsylvania 17201.

Preface

WHAT DILIGENT scholars of the Theravāda Buddhist tradition know is not always what they communicate in writing; what serious students need to know about this tradition is frequently inaccessible. A curious situation has occurred in which the threefold refuge (*tisaraṇa*) or triple gem (*tiratana*), the formulation of which is a central dimension of the Theravāda Buddhist tradition, has remained relatively unfocused in Western literature because, perhaps, so pervasively assumed by Buddhists.

These essays bring into focal awareness, in a form readily available in the West, one of the oldest formulaic expressions of faith in human history, one which remains vibrant and widespread today: the threefold refuge, the triple gem. This volume represents an initial move upon which others can build and, it is hoped, move beyond. In the meantime, in which we do our living and our thinking, the authors trust that what we have brought together will contribute to an increasingly more adequate understanding of the religious heritage of Theravāda Buddhists.

The original drafts for the chapters of this volume were first shared as presentations to professional societies in the course of a little more than a decade. The chapter by Edmund F. Perry and Shanta Ratnayaka (Chapter IV) was first on the scene, published in 1974, and made available to the other contributors shortly thereafter. The next was Chapter I by John Ross Carter, published in 1979. In February of the same year a paper resulting in Chapter III was presented by Carter at the Midwest regional meeting of the American Academy of Religion held at Northwestern University. A cumulative process was launched and in the fall of 1979, George D. Bond presented a preliminary version of Chapter II at the annual meeting of the American Academy of Religion.

There has been no attempt to organize a task force, as it were, to hold conferences for the authors in order to construct a carefully collaborated presentation. Although there are differences in English style and in choice of English equivalents for Pāli terms, the presentations in the chapters cohere in the common subject, and the particular orientations and concerns represent legitimate ramifications of the subject.

For this volume, two appendixes have been included as aids for readers interested in pursuing the subject and related matters. Appendix I, written and arranged by John Ross Carter, is designed to enable a person, who does not have access to literature in the Pāli language, to locate Pāli textual passages related to the subject of this volume in English translations. Appendix II, written and compiled by Geoge D. Bond, lists the major Pāli commentaries with their corresponding canonical collections and provides a ready reference for persons who might wish to pursue further studies in Pāli canonical and commentarial sources of the Theravāda tradition.

We wish to thank Elizabeth H. Davey, Secretary to the Director of the Fund for the Study of the Great Religions, Colgate University, for her methodical care in typing the final copy for publication. And the editor is grateful for the cheerful enthusiasm and supportive efficiency of the colleague-authors of this volume.

John Ross Carter

Colgate University

Table of Contents

THE THREEFOLD REFUGE

I go to the Buddha as refuge;
I go to Dhamma as refuge;
I go to the Sangha as refuge.

For the second time, I go to the Buddha as refuge;
For the second time, I go to Dhamma as refuge;
For the second time, I go to the Sangha as refuge.

For the third time, I go to the Buddha as refuge;
For the third time, I go to Dhamma as refuge;
For the third time, I go to the Sangha as refuge.

Buddhaṃ saraṇaṃ gacchāmi
dhammaṃ saraṇaṃ gacchāmi
saṃghaṃ saraṇaṃ gacchāmi

Dutiyam pi buddhaṃ saraṇaṃ gacchāmi
dutiyam pi dhammaṃ saraṇaṃ gacchāmi
dutiyam pi saṃghaṃ saraṇaṃ gacchāmi.

Tatiyam pi buddhaṃ saraṇaṃ gacchāmi
tatiyam pi dhammaṃ saraṇaṃ gacchāmi
tatiyam pi saṃghaṃ saraṇaṃ gacchāmi.

Khuddaka-Pāṭha, p. 1.

1 The Notion of Refuge (*Saraṇa*) in the Theravāda Buddhist Tradition[1]

John Ross Carter

FOR MANY CENTURIES Buddhist men and women – monks, nuns, and laity – have taken refuge (*saraṇa*), found refuge in the Buddha, in Dhamma, and in the Sangha.[2] At first glance a notion of refuge might suggest a passive, retrogressive move, a retreat, a withdrawal; and one might interpret this as corroborating an interpretation that "Buddhism is world-denying or world-negating."

Buddhists have demonstrated otherwise; they have entered into commerce, have written poetry, have dug canals and tanks for irrigation, have tried to minimize overhead and increase profits, have frequented royal courts, have given to the poor, have coped with famine, have celebrated colorful festivals. Very little withdrawal is manifested here – and yet Buddhists have participated in these activities while taking refuge.

The notion of refuge is both delicate and complicated. Perhaps many who have seen themselves as part of the Buddhist community have given little thought to what is meant when one chooses to take refuge in the triple gem: the Buddha, Dhamma, the Sangha. Yet, others, in one way or another, have thought about it, and it is largely due to their efforts that one can note the presence of Buddhists living in the world today.

Buddhists have said that refuge (*saraṇa*) is like a cave (*leṇa*), like a protective enclosure (*tāṇa*). At the same time they have stressed that refuge is not a passive matter, a recoiling in the face of the world(s). Rather, it seems their point has been that this refuge provides a recourse, a source of aid. When one finds this refuge one is not fleeing from the world; rather, one is entering a process of transcending. Simultaneously with a discernment that one has found refuge, it would seem, there is a recognition that the world is defined (*definire*), limited. So the movement into refuge, this protective enclosure, represents an understanding that one is moving onwards in a liberating process because the world has been placed into a meaningful context, i.e., defined.

Very early in the Buddhist movement the notion of going for refuge, taking refuge, was made the standard, formalized expression representing a new relationship which was the consequence of a profoundly personal reorientation of one's life. It appears that at an early stage of the Buddhist movement, refuge was taken in the Buddha as the glorious exemplar (*Bhagavan*), and Dhamma as the supportive process of living well and the supportive ideal, i.e., salvific Truth. Those who made this move and professed this commitment, confessed this protection, were called, in the *Vinaya*, "two-word-ones" (*dvevācikā*).[3] Theravāda Buddhists, in the course of centuries, have tended not to forget this early historical setting, and so a reader is reminded of the early two-fold formula in the commentary on the *Jātaka*,[4] in the *Upāsakajanālaṅkāra* (13th century),[5] and in a Sinhalese text, the *Śrī Saddharmāvavāda Saṃgrahaya* (18th century).[6] A Sinhalese glossary of the Jātaka commentary, the *Jātaka Aṭuvā Gätapadaya* (12th century-?) provides an obvious explanation for the two-fold formula, "because the Sangha-gem had not arisen in the world."[7]

Rather soon in the history of the Buddhist movement, a threefold formula became established and, for centuries, has remained the standard expression representing one's reorientation. Also in the *Vinaya*, one meets the word *tevācika*, ("three-word-one,") used to designate a person who had found refuge in the *Bhagavan*, Dhamma, and the *bhikkhusaṅgha*.[8] The commentarial tradition has been consistent in insisting on the regularity of the triple refuge; that refuge is found in the Buddha, Dhamma, and the Sangha. On occasion when the canonical texts mention praise only of the Buddha and Dhamma, the commentaries remind the reader of the standard expression for praising the Sangha.[9]

In the course of time, the term *Buddha* became standard in this formula, and it appears *sāvakasaṅgha,* in a comprehensive sense designating all those persons, the eight noble persons, engaged in a process that leads to liberation, was also used along with *bhikkhusaṅgha,* which designated the order of monks. In time, Theravāda Buddhists preferred an interpretation of the Sangha in the three-fold refuge to mean the community of disciples (*sāvakas*) who had made the breakthrough into Dhamma, who had entered the stream — in short, those realizing the effectiveness of the way characterized as having four paths and four fruits with Nibbāna as the culmination. Apparently, Theravāda Buddhists have been aware for quite some time that institutions, the status of being a *bhikkhu,* a monk, that rites and rituals, what some Western scholars tend to mean when they write about something called "Buddhism," in themselves are not an adequate basis for refuge.[10]

Frequently the term *gems* or *jewels* is used to designate the Buddha, Dhamma, and the Sangha; hence, one speaks of the triple gem, or *tiratana* (three gems or jewels). The commentary on the *Khuddakapātha* elaborates the meaning of *ratana* ("gem or jewel") as follows: "*Ratana* is a synonym for that which induces, brings, produces, increases delight (*rati*), for whatever is valued, very costly, inestimable, rarely seen, having incomparable enjoyment for beings."[11]

In considering the relationship Buddhists have continually discerned in the Buddha, Dhamma, and the Sangha, one becomes aware that for Buddhists this relationship is one of delightful refuge, joyful protection.

What, then, is meant by going for refuge? The commentarial tradition provides a seven-fold classification.

> For the sake of proficiency in the acts of going for refuge, this classification should be understood: namely [1] refuge, [2] the going for refuge, [3] the one who goes for refuge, [4] the mode of going for refuge, [5] the effect of going for refuge, [6] defilement, and [7] breach [of the going for refuge].[12]

And why is this called refuge? Note the dynamic thrust of what follows:

> 'Refuge' (*saraṇa*) is so called because it slays (*hiṃsati*), such is the force of the term. Of those who have gone for refuge, by just this act of going for refuge, it [*i.e., saraṇa*] slays, it destroys fear, affliction, *dukkha*, and misery of unsatisfactory [future] abodes. This [*i.e., saraṇa*] is a synonym for the three gems themselves.
>
> In other words, the Buddha, by causing the performance of what is beneficial and by causing one to turn from what is not beneficial, destroys fear on the part of beings. And Dhamma, by causing one to cross over the wilderness of becoming, by giving consolation [destroys fear], and the Sangha, by causing even those who have done little to derive great benefits [destroys fear]. Therefore in this manner are the three gems a refuge.[13]

Going for refuge, taking refuge, discovering refuge represents a lively religious awareness demonstrated by Theravāda Buddhists. When this credal statement is pondered, a reflective person might recall the moment when first he found the statement true and because the triple refuge is frequently uttered a person has repeated occasions to determine whether he is being consistent. The triple refuge can be said either in a private setting or in public, as a part of a corporate religious service. In any setting, the process involved is deeply personal. The recitation of the triple refuge is ritually structured in a threefold repetition to develop reflective alertness. This repetitive pattern sets the expression apart from routine patterns in normal discourse, serves to check a participant from running roughshod through a communal affirmation that has echoed through history, and tends to engender a sense of thoroughness in personal involvement.

Part of what it means to live religiously is to discover that in so living one is engaged in a process of transcending, in the widest sense; transcending what one has known, how one has thought, what one has been, how one has lived. Theravāda Buddhists have attested that in this process of transcending there is an exemplar (the Buddha); there is his testimony (dhamma) that Truth (Dhamma) is salvific; and there is a crowd of witnesses, those disciples (*sāvakasaṅgha*) who have entered and gone far in the paths that fructify (a mixed metaphor that falls sharply into focus in the lives of persons); and there is the monastic order that has contributed to continuity within the tradition (*bhikkhusaṅgha*).

One has not begun to understand what going for refuge

(*saraṇagamana*) has meant to Theravāda Buddhists without taking seriously their affirmation that anxieties and pressures can be extinguished thereby and that a fragmented life can be made whole. The commentarial tradition has long known the human predicament, subtly held in the notion of *dukkha*, and it is noteworthy that going for refuge is said to slay, put an end to this *dukkha*. We are on to something weighty here. *Dukkha* "reflects a meaning of disarrangement, disorientation, disorder, being disjointed, and through extension, discontent, discord, and 'disease,' concerning the physical (*kāyikadukkha*) and mental (*mānasadukkha*) dimensions of life, individually and socially considered."[14] To say that *dukkha* suggests "the world is out of joint"[15] or "all life is awry"[16] would be on the mark. And all of this is sensed as causing oppression (*paṭipiḷana*).[17]

So the movement involved in going for refuge represents a process of putting an end to *dukkha*. For such a person the world becomes defined, placed into perspective; fear of the future and bitterness for the past are put at rest; purpose for living is discerned, and a mode of conduct remarkably consistent with this purpose is endorsed. On the deepest level, going for refuge represents an orientation to transcendence as goal and as process in which one's personality is holistically integrated in the commonality of living beings, in community among men and women.

A delicate transformation occurs when one goes for refuge, a transformation within the person that enables him no longer to rail with disoriented frustration against a world that is out of joint, no longer to whimper because all life is awry, no longer to engage in a Grand Revolt against meaninglessness, which, it is said, enables some to live meaningfully, but, rather, now to live with an admirable composure that reflects an awareness of the efficacy of a gospel message, now to instill order where there is disorder, to heal the wounds of life, to put an end to *dukkha*. *Dukkha* can be terminated. This is part of the gospel; *dukkha* is antepenultimate.

A reader of the Pāli commentaries learns that going for refuge is not merely a ritual that a Buddhist does, or a bit of liturgy that some people perform. The commentaries tell the reader to turn his attention to what one might call the seat of emotions, even the heart (*citta*), to look there in order to discern the depth of the thoughts involved in this going for refuge:

> The going for refuge is the arousing of thoughts (*cittuppāda*), which are free of defilement by virtue of being gladdened in it [going for refuge] and showing respect for it, which are activated by reason of being inclined to it. It is a being endowed with this [going for refuge] that does go for refuge.[18]

Nor are we dealing here with what one might consider merely an inchoate religious awareness, an incipient emotional sensitivity. The commentarial tradition has interpreted this going, this movement, as an activity of knowing, of understanding.

> Whatever [philological] roots convey the meaning of 'going' convey also the meaning of 'knowing' (*buddhi*). Hence, for this [expression] 'I go' the meaning 'I know, I understand' is expressed.[19]

A person who is inclined to go for refuge, who considers going for refuge a weighty matter,who makes the commitment with a pure and joyous heart and mind enters a process of knowing, of deepening understanding of himself, his neighbor, his world and that which transcends the world.

So refuge, the going for refuge, and the person who goes for refuge are three elements inseparably fused in a momentous religious experience.

The commentarial discussion also provides an explanation of the modes of going for refuge, and it does this by introducing two fundamental categories, a *lokuttara* going for refuge and a *lokiya* going for refuge. These two terms, *lokuttara* and *lokiya*, are well known to students of Pāli and have been frequently translated as "transcendental" (*lokuttara*) and "mundane" (*lokiya*). It might come as a surprise to some for one to suggest that in reflecting on the meaning of refuge the latter term, *lokiya*, seemed to be the more problematic to translate adequately. As contrasting terms, one might say whatever *lokiya* means, *lokuttara* somehow transcends, goes beyond (*uttara*) the world(s) (*loka, lokiya*) and hence one occasionally finds *lokuttara* translated as "supramundane."

Loka, the noun, has a broad spectrum of meaning but basically it means "world" or "realm" and also "people" or "humankind." In most cases *lokiya*, the derivative adjective, means "like the world," *i.e.*, common, ordinary, usual, customary, and hence has been translated as "mundane." To describe something as mundane suggests that it somehow has to do with human activity that in most cases has a practical orientation that is concerned with the immediate situation, which is, like the world, transient and which is, like the world, common, ordinary. Some might interpret *mundane* as having to do with things of the world with little or no concern for the ideal or for what is heavenly.

To use the term *mundane* in attempting to communicate what is involved in the activity that Theravāda Buddhists have called *lokiyasaraṇagamana* or *lokiya*, going for refuge, might be misleading. Western students of the Theravāda tradition are well aware of the attitudes expressed by Theravāda men and women about the ultimate objective in living. Ordinarily, Buddhologists tend to speak of this objective as Nibbāna, though I prefer to represent it as Dhamma/Nibbāna. It is difficult to overstress the significance of this objective for Theravāda Buddhist men and women or the impact of this vision on the religious history of humankind generally. Yet in stressing the ultimacy of this objective and the centrality of this pursuit within the Theravāda tradition, one might tend to underrate the legitimate religious expression involved in the *lokiya* going for refuge. Making it peripheral or merely secondary, one might then interpret this going for refuge as merely mundane.

Buddhists have seen this world in which we are living as part of a larger whole, as one world among many. Some worlds, or plains of existence, are more enjoyable than this one, some are much worse, and a person is where he or she is because of past deeds. Where one will be depends on how one lives now – this is sobering. Buddhists have spoken of the justice perceived in one's coursing through the worlds as integrally related to how one lives and thinks, *i.e.*, one's *kamma*. Buddhists have come to discern that *kamma*, volitional activity expressed in body, mind, and speech, is set in a context in which justice reigns; a context in which a concomitant subtle presence of righteousness and mercy (*i.e.*, it is a context not arbitrary, whimsical, despotic, chaotic, nor is there fate) seem to be acknowledged. In this setting *kamma* represents an affirmation that a moral order (*dhamma*) abides, that we reap what we sow; wholesomeness in so far as our intentions and actions are in accordance with Dhamma or detrimental consequences in so far as our intentions and actions are divergent from Dhamma. Lest one consider the notion of *kamma* to be a "theory" of impressive intellectual cogency only, Buddhists have tried to make the point that faith (*saddhā*) is involved. One puts one's heart (*saddahati*)[20] in the moral significance of volitional activity and one sets about to arrange one's life in accordance with the norm that volitional activities yield consequences.[21] And, of course, the *lokiya* going for refuge yields significant consequences in this world and in the future in the other worlds.

Fortunately, we are not without instructive testimony about what is involved in this *lokiya* going for refuge. The commentarial discussion says,

> The *lokiya* going for refuge is this; by arresting whatever defiles the going for refuge on the part of the average person it [*lokiya* going for refuge] takes on the virtues of the Buddha *etc.* [Dhamma, Sangha] to be its objective and flourishes in this way. In effect, it means the attainment of faith (*saddhā*) in the Buddha and the other subjects [Dhamma, Sangha]. Proper vision conditioned by faith is called straight conduct following from proper views and this pertains to the ten fields of meritorious action. That [proper action with regard to the subjects, Buddha, Dhamma, and Sangha] functions in four modes: [1] by the dedication of oneself, [2] by being inclined to them, [3] by undertaking the state of a pupil, [4] by prostration.[22]

In a brief transitional passage introduced by the commentary the reader is struck by two phrases that occur in the brief statements used to catch the force of the four modes being considered here.[23] Firstly, one meets "from today onwards," and one is placed face to face with the seriousness of the dedication, the orientation, the discipleship, and prostration. Persons are putting their lives on the line. Secondly, this is not exclusively a private matter, though it is deeply personal. One reads the phrase "you all consider (*dhāretha*) me as one who has done thusly," and this public dimension adds to the totality of the commitment in the person, and the person senses the buttressing influence of others by his movement into a religious community.

With impressive conciseness the commentary, following a long established procedure in Theravāda hermeneutics, quotes passages from the older literature. In this way one who goes for refuge is enabled to interpret one's own activity as a participation in a communal continuity of faith.

(1) Dedication:

And also I dedicate myself to the *Bhagavan*, I dedicate myself to Dhamma and to the Sangha, and my life I dedicate, dedicated indeed is myself, dedicated also is my life even until the end of my life. I go for refuge to the Buddha. The Buddha is my refuge, shelter, protection.[24]

(2) The state of a resident pupil:

And indeed I would see the teacher (*satthar*), I would see only the *Bhagavan*, and I would see the One Well-gone (*sugata*), I would see only the *Bhagavan*. And indeed I would see the *Sammāsambuddha*, I would see only the *Bhagavan*.[25]

This preceding passage is quoted from the *Saṃyuttanikāya* and there the original continues,

> And then I, having fallen prostrate at the feet of the *Bhagavan* thusly, said to the *Bhagavan*, "Sir, my teacher (*satthar*) is the *Bhagavan*, I am his disciple."[26]

(3) On inclination:

Thus I will wander from village to village,
From town to town,
Revering the *Sambuddha*
And the excellent reliability of Dhamma (*dhammassasudhammatam*).[27]

(4) On prostration:

Now Brahmāyu, a brahman, stood up from his seat, placed the outer robe on his shoulder, bowed his head to the feet of the *Bhagavan* and [now] covers the feet of the *Bhagavan* with kisses with his mouth and strokes [them] with his hands and announces his name, saying, 'I am, O Gotama, Brahmāyu, a brahman, I am, O Gotama, Brahmāyu, a brahman.'[28]

The commentarial discussion does not intend to suggest different ways of *lokiya* going for refuge, or different levels or steps, with an assumption that a Buddhist is to see himself at any one time as participating in one and not the others.[29] Rather, it appears that the discussion works along the line of a "this too" principle, a principle of inclusion; this, too, is a way of going for refuge, as is noted in this or that passage, and further, this, too, is a dimension of a person's personal interpretation of what is involved in his activity of going for refuge on, perhaps, the first occasion some years ago and even now, today.

The commentarial tradition has made a significant contribution to the continuity of the tradition in which the commentator participated. With regard to the notion of going for refuge the commentators drew together strands of religious awareness embedded in passages scattered throughout the canonical literature not only because the strands were there to be collected but also, and profoundly I think, because these strands had been interwoven in the lives of Buddhists for quite some time. It would seem that for centuries men and women have sat at the feet of *bhikkhus*, who utilized the commentarial discussion in preaching Dhamma, and have been inspired by an exhortation to dedicate their lives, to study and to learn, to trust the reliability of Dhamma in the context of loving devotion springing not from a state of frenzy but from a calm heart delicately quickened with a delightful sense of being taken up.

The attitude suggested by the act of prostration in going for refuge has been further interpreted by considering what constitutes proper motivation for obeisance. The commentarial tradition makes the point quite clearly that family loyalty is no basis for going for refuge, neither is fear of retribution, nor an appreciation for practical benefits imparted by one's instructor (*ācariya*). Rather, the discernment of the inherent incomparable worthiness of the one before whom prostration is made (*i.e.*, the Buddha) provides the proper motivation.[30] And further, prostration before others as a socially sanctioned gesture of respect does not, in this case, constitute a breach in commitment involved in going for refuge. Consequently the commentarial tradition notes that paying homage to one's elder relatives, even should it be the case that an elder relative has become committed to the way of another religious teacher and tradition, does not rupture the commitment of going for refuge. Similarly, when homage motivated by fear is paid to a great king and when homage motivated by sincere appreciation is paid to an instructor (*ācariya*) who has imparted the skills of a craft, even though this instructor be committed to the way of another religious teacher and tradition, no rupture occurs in the commitment of going for refuge.[31]

The *lokiya* going for refuge is certainly a religious act; we have noticed the seriousness of the activity, the presence of faith, the sense of a lifelong commitment to the eradication of *dukkha*, the discernment of the inherent worthiness of that which constitutes this refuge, among other things. There is, further, an affirmation that living one's life in accordance with the commitment to and confidence in this refuge leads to a better life in this world and in worlds to come in the future. The commentarial tradition reminds one that being faithful to this refuge has as its effect the enjoyment of future existence among the gods and the enjoyment of plenty.[32]

Ignorance, doubt, and misapprehension with regard to the Buddha, Dhamma, and the Sangha taint this *lokiya* going for refuge and, consequently, inhibit the effulgence of the religious awareness and the efflorescence of the experience in one's life now and in the future. And the continuity of the commitment can be ruptured by devoting oneself, as depicted in this going for refuge, to another religious teacher and upon death. In the former case, the breach in the continuity of commitment is censurable and carries with it unfavorable consequences. In the latter case, the act of death itself, being without volition or desire, yields no consequence, and consequently this act causing a breach in this commitment is blameless.

Such is the *lokiya* going for refuge. Is this going for refuge mundane? Yes and no. It is mundane in the Buddhist sense in so far as taking refuge in this way will enable one to live in a process of transcending but a process, nevertheless, not finally transcending the worlds, *i.e.*, *saṃsāra*, the whirl of (*vaṭṭa*) existence as Buddhists customarily speak of it. However, the *lokiya* going for refuge is not mundane as some Westerners might tend to understand what is usually considered mundane. *Lokiyasaraṇagamana*, *lokiya* going for refuge, is not in opposition to what might be considered spiritual or lofty as the term *mundane* might suggest. Nor is *lokiya* going for refuge to be viewed as a practical activity — again as the term *mundane* might suggest — an activity that is primarily considered useful. This activity of going for refuge is praised for being beneficial; yet, for one to pose as having taken refuge for this reason, because it is useful for making better one's station in life, would be to overlook, indeed not to see, the swift pungent reminder that craving (*taṅhā*) and greed (*lobha*), in whatever conceptual garb they might be disguised, drag one downward, cause one to stumble, check a process of transcending.

Perhaps one might suggest "customary"[33] as an English concept bordering on adequacy for the Pāli word *lokiya* in *lokiyasaraṇagamana*, recognizing that what are customary forms of religious expression for one community might strike an observer as remarkably engaging and profoundly significant. A Westerner might catch the force of *lokiya* in *lokiyasaraṇagamana* by interpreting *lokiya* to mean "heavenly," keeping in mind that Buddhists have apperceived the heavens to be a part of *saṃsāra*, and remembering that Buddhists have discerned a higher stage in the process of transcending, one called *lokuttara*. Consequently, one might understand the relationship between the adjectives *lokiya* and *lokuttara* as roughly homologous to "heavenly" and "godly" in Western religious terminology. To speak of *lokiya* in the context of going for refuge as representing an activity that is mundane or worldly might tend to lead a Westerner, a non-Buddhist, not to be aware of the lively religious emotion and active commitment to a way of life that is with purpose, that is integrative, that seeks to alleviate *dukkha* in one's life and in the world.

There is another dimension of going for refuge, one that is transcendental, a *lokuttarasaraṇagamana*, a going for refuge that transcends the world(s), this world *and* the heavens. One is told that this transcendental going for refuge has as its consequence not the attainment of the heavens, but the realization of the four fruitions of one striving for inward calm (*samaṇa*): stream entrance, once-returner, non-returner, and *arahant*. This going for refuge has as its reward not the acquisition of plenty, but, rather, the destruction of all *dukkha*.[34]

Such *lokuttara* going for refuge occurs when one has had a vision of the truths, which is concomitant to the moment of entering the path (*maggakkhaṇa*), together with a complete cutting off[35] of what harms this going for refuge. The objective is the realization of Nibbāna,[36] (*Dhamma/Nibbāna*) which is synonymous with a penetration of Dhamma, salvific Truth. This realization, this penetration provided the basis for the virtuous qualities of the Buddha, continues to provide a corroboration of the virtuous qualities of Dhamma, and yields in the lives of the *sāvakasaṅgha* an increasing pervasiveness of virtuous qualities as these noble persons penetrate Dhamma more deeply, realize Nibbāna more fully.

Proper insight into the four noble truths is of utmost importance in this transcendental going for refuge. The commentarial tradition quotes from the *Dhammapada,*

> He who has gone to the Buddha and Dhamma and the Sangha
> Sees by proper insight (*sammāpaññā*) the four noble truths:
> *Dukkha,* the arising of *dukkha,* and the overcoming of *dukkha,*
> And the noble eightfold path that leads to the quieting of *dukkha.*
> Indeed, this is the refuge that is tranquil, this is the highest refuge (*etaṃ saraṇaṃ uttamaṃ*).
> Having come to this refuge, he is released from all *dukkha.*[37]

The reward of this transcendental going for refuge is the termination of regarding certain conditions as permanent. The commentarial tradition again provides a quotation,

> This, O *bhikkhus,* is impossible, that a person possessed of [proper] view [*i.e.,* stream attainer] would regard any psychophysical synergy (*saṅkhāra*) as permanent (*nicca*), would regard them as blissful (*sukha*), would regard any *dhamma* as self (*atta*),[38] would deprive his mother of life, would deprive his father of life, would deprive an *arahant* of life . . . would with a corrupt heart draw the blood of the *Tathāgata,* would cause disunity in the Sangha, would turn towards another teacher; this cannot take place.[39]

On reading this quotation one might wonder why it was chosen to elaborate what is involved in *lokuttara* going for refuge — indeed, murder is a stunning transgression of the commitment involved even in the customary (*lokiya*) going for refuge by one who takes seriously the first precept of virtue, (*sīla*), *i.e.,* to refrain from taking life. The passage was probably chosen firstly to elaborate the integral relationship of the three characteristics of sentient existence (*tilakkhaṇa*) — that all *saṅkhāras* are fleeting (*anicca*), awry (*dukkha*) and that all processes (*dhammas*) are without self (*anatta*) — with the four noble truths. Secondly, the commentary is working in the realm of *certainty* and doing so by quoting a passage from the *Aṅguttara-nikāya* (I, 26-27) enumerating patterns of behavior resolutely dissociated from the behavior of one possessed of proper vision. The point is straightforward and is made with full confidence — the transcendental going for refuge is never soiled by misapprehension nor is it ever ruptured.

> There is not at all a rupture of the transcendental [going for refuge]. Even in the transition from one life to another the noble disciple does not propose another teacher.[40]

Were there a possibility of a rupture in the transcendental going for refuge, there would remain a gap of sorts within the Theravāda soteriological vision, a zone of uncertainty engendered by a recognition of man's capacity to delude himself, crowning himself ruler of his future by the exercise of his will. It appears that Buddhists are affirming that one does not take refuge in one's will because one knows oneself well enough to realize oneself as other than the source of liberation. There is no need of a savior, as Buddhists continually remind one, not because man is his own savior but because of the efficacy of Dhamma when made the integral basis of one's life.

Nor would there be a need to quest for another teacher. In the customary mode of going for refuge (*lokiyasaraṇagamana*) one is to maintain a loyalty to the Buddha as one's teacher. In the transcendental mode of going for refuge (*lokuttarasaraṇagamana*) one has already penetrated that about which the teacher taught, that which will lead onward, will not fail, and is sufficient to meet every situation. When one recognizes that this breakthrough has occurred, it is not necessary to look for another teacher. One does not consider abandoning this process of living, nor think of standing in the way of others who are engaged with similar pursuits. Such would be inconceivable.

Refuge, although elaborated within the tradition as three-fold, is one. And for Buddhists it is not locked within the vicissitudes of history — we are. But because there is refuge, persons who discern that refuge are thereby enabled to transcend the vicissitudes of history or *saṃsāra*, as some of us view the situation, not because history or *saṃsāra* has changed but because persons have changed.

The study of the life of the Buddha, the four noble truths, dependent origination, *kamma*, the monastic institution, and so on, is, indeed, important. However, such study would yield little that is momentous for the history of a religious community, which has participated in and has perpetuated an impressive religious tradition, without an understanding of what Buddhists have discerned in the notion of refuge (*saraṇa*).

2 The Buddha as Refuge
in the Theravāda Buddhist Tradition[1]

George D. Bond

Some Western scholars and some modern Buddhists themselves depict Theravāda Buddhism as a religion of individual salvation-striving. No one has expressed and reinforced this stereotype better than Max Weber, who wrote of the Buddhism of the Pāli canon, "Buddhism represents the most radical form of salvation-striving conceivable. Its salvation is a solely personal act of the single individual. There is no recourse to a deity or savior."[2]

Like most stereotypes, this one contains some truth, but it also fails to express important dimensions and nuances of the tradition. We recognize the difficulty with this view of the Theravāda tradition when we consider the three refuges (*tisaraṇa*). If one maintains that the Theravāda tradition represents "a religion of individual salvation-striving," one would be hard pressed to provide an explanation for the devotional element represented by the three refuges. Nevertheless, from ancient times to the present Buddhists have sought refuge in the Buddha, the Dhamma, and the Sangha. Moreover, they have regarded "going for refuge" (*saraṇagamana*) not as an empty ritual but as a meaningful religious act integral to the way of salvation.[3]

In this chapter we consider the first of these refuges, the Buddha as refuge, by examining its meaning in the Pāli canonical texts and commentaries. This refuge seems most problematic on Weber's interpretation and raises most pointedly the question of the place of devotion in the Theravāda tradition.[4] Therefore the questions that will concern us here are (1) What is the religious significance of refuge in the Buddha; how does going for refuge in the Buddha solve the human predicament? (2) Did the Buddha liberate beings or teach that each being must strive for its own individual salvation?

The act of going to the Buddha for refuge seems to have been part of the Buddhist tradition almost from the outset. To be sure, the Theravāda tradition relates that Gotama occasionally rebuffed the flattery and fawning admiration of some of his followers. He silenced Sāriputta's praise of him as the greatest being that ever lived by asking sharply whether Sāriputta had known all the enlightened beings of the past, present and future with whom he compared the Buddha.[5] When Vakkali expressed his pleasure at the sight of the Buddha, the Buddha directed him instead to the Dhamma saying, "He who sees the Dhamma, sees me; and he who sees me sees the Dhamma."[6] Like a true teacher, the Buddha said that seeing and following the Dhamma was the highest form of worship one could offer him.[7]

But the texts also relate both that the natural reaction of people who came in contact with the Buddha was veneration by seeking refuge and that the Buddha did not reject this devotion. According to the tradition, the first and the last persons who met Gotama during his lifetime responded to him and his teaching by going for refuge in him.[8] Far from disapproving of this response, the Buddha established the three refuges as the formula to be used in the first ordination ritual.[9] The commentarial tradition explains further that the three refuges constitute the path by which all beings enter the Buddha's dispensation (*sāsana*) whether to become members of the Sangha or lay-followers.[10] Throughout the canon we find that as a standard conclusion to many of the Buddha's dialogues the people addressed in the dialogue go for refuge in him and request that he accept them as lay-followers, *upāsakas*, or *bhikkhus*. So standard is this response that it usually occurs in a fixed form: having seen and heard the Buddha, a person exclaims,

> Excellent Venerable Gotama, Excellent Venerable Gotama. It is as if one were to set upright that which had been turned over, or were to uncover that which had been hidden . . . thus in many ways the Dhamma has been made known by the Venerable Gotama. Therefore I go for refuge to the Blessed Gotama, and to the Dhamma, and

> the Sangha. May the Venerable Gotama accept me as a lay follower/monk who from this day forward, as long as life lasts, has gone for refuge.[11]

In some *suttas* we find a significant variation on this response. When the teacher in a *sutta* is one of the Buddha's chief disciples, like Mahā Kaccāna, rather than Gotama himself, at the conclusion of the disciple's teaching the hearer proclaims *via* this same formula that he wishes to go for refuge to Mahā Kaccāna or whichever disciple has been the subject of the *sutta*. In these cases, the disciple states clearly that the person cannot go for refuge to him but should go for refuge only to the Buddha, the one who is the supreme refuge for all.[12]

This refusal by Mahā Kaccāna and other disciples to accept the devotion of lay-followers, a refusal to allow people to go for refuge to anyone except Gotama, raises some important questions. One question, which we cannot digress very far to explore, is why would lay people request to go to the disciples for refuge? What was the ordinary person's conception of refuge? That the monks are said to have refused such requests sounds a note prominent in the later development of the Theravāda tradition. Throughout the history of this tradition the Sangha has been largely anonymous in that its leaders refused to allow personality cults to develop and refrained from building their own empires. Like other religious traditions and monastic communities, the Theravāda Sangha has surely comprised many brilliant philosophers, textual scholars, preachers, and others with outstanding talent and leadership ability. But the chronicles and commentaries tell us almost nothing about them. Consistently, it seems, Theravāda *bhikkhus* have pointed beyond themselves to the Buddha and the Dhamma. This leads us to ask, what sets the Buddha apart and establishes him as the only figure worthy of being a refuge? Why should people go for refuge to the Buddha rather than to an enlightened disciple or someone else?

Perhaps the most concise answer to this question is found in one of the Buddha's dialogues in which he declares that "With regard to [the whole world of] gods and men, he who is endowed with wisdom and virtuous conduct is the best (*seṭṭha*)."[13] The Buddha goes on to explain that he is the *seṭṭha*, the most excellent being in the world, because he has attained perfection of this kind. The Pāli commentaries, handed down by those anonymous Theravāda elders and compiled by Buddhaghosa, expand upon this tradition of the authority of the Buddha as refuge. The *Khuddaka-Pāṭha* commentary, *Paramatthajotikā I*, employs a definition from the *Niddesa* as a summary of what the term *Buddha* means in the refuge formula: "'Buddha' means he is that Exalted One who is self-become, who is without a teacher in things (*dhammas*) not heard before, who himself attained the highest wisdom of the truths and therein reached omniscience and mastery over the fruitions."[14] The *Visuddhimagga* offers another concise explanation of the ways in which the Buddha is the "best," a being set apart from other human beings. This explanation, almost creedal in form, also originated in the canonical texts and continues to live in the Theravāda tradition, where every ceremony and every reaffirmation of the three refuges inevitably includes this "salutation to the Buddha." It defines and praises the Buddha as having nine special qualities:

> The Exalted One is worthy (*arahaṃ*), fully enlightened (*sammāsambuddho*), endowed with wisdom and virtuous conduct (*vijjācaraṇasampanno*), well-gone (*sugato*), the knower of the worlds (*lokavidū*), unsurpassed charioteer of men to be tamed (*anuttaro purisadammasārathi*), teacher of gods and men (*satthā devamanussānaṃ*), an Enlightened One (*Buddho*), the Exalted One (*Bhagavā*).[15]

The commentators reflected on this concise salutation with detailed explanations of these and other attributes that set the Buddha apart as the only being who is a suitable object for refuge.

We can summarize the commentarial explanations by grouping the Buddha's distinctive qualities under four headings.

(1) He is said to have attained the highest spiritual perfection, which in the Indian religious context meant developing wisdom or insight into the ultimate Truth and overcoming all the mental, physical, and emotional defilements and hindrances that obstruct the path to perfection for ordinary beings. The commentaries and canonical texts use many terms to describe Gotama's wisdom. He is said to have possessed omniscience (*sabbaññutā* or *sabbavidū*).[16] He is all-seeing and of great wisdom (*mahāpaññā*).[17] In the salutation to the Buddha, seven of the nine terms relate, in whole or in part, to Gotama's perfection in wisdom. As one fully

enlightened (*sammāsambuddha*), he has realized all dhammas rightly; he has seen and analyzed the truth about existence. Explaining the term, *sammāsambuddha*, the *Vissuddhimagga* lists as the content of Gotama's knowledge all the various categories of the teachings (the *pariyatti-dhamma*).[18] As a Buddha and an Exalted One (*bhagavant*), he has reached perfection of wisdom (*vijjā*) by becoming an *arahant*, and one well-gone (*sugata*). The expression, knower of worlds (*lokavidū*), denotes his total knowledge of all beings and all world systems.[19] In general, the Buddha has attained supreme wisdom and in one text is called *veda*, which, I. B. Horner has suggested, "may mean that he is Knowledge itself."[20]

The Buddha could not have reached this lofty peak of wisdom, however, without traversing all the lower levels of the path, perfecting his life in the world and conquering his mind. Therefore, the tradition relates that Gotama had destroyed the defilements (*kilesas*) and the intoxications (*āsavas*) that cloud the mind and prevent most people from seeing or striving for ultimate reality.[21] His senses restrained, his desires severed, his vision clear, the Buddha fulfilled the ideals of ethical conduct (*sīla*) and concentration (*samādhi, jhāna*) in order to reach the wisdom (*paññā*) that brings ultimate liberation.[22]

(2) To these spiritual accomplishments, this realization of the Truth, the tradition adds one further fact that heightens and magnifies the Buddha's achievement: Gotama reached this goal by himself without a teacher. The commentators explained the term *sammāsambuddha* by analyzing it etymologically[23] to mean "he has understood (*buddha*) all things rightly (*sammā*) by himself (*sāmaṃ*)."[24] In almost every instance in which the Buddha's enlightenment is discussed, mention is also made of his being self-enlightened. He is described as "without teacher in things (*dhammas*) not heard before" and as one who "alone discovered the supreme complete enlightenment."[25] To the ascetic Upaka, Gotama proclaims, "There is no teacher for me, one equal to me does not exist."[26] For Buddhists, the Buddha is not just enlightened, he is self-enlightened (*sayambhū*); and the combination of these two factors establishes the Buddha's authority and his significance as a refuge.

(3) Because of this dual accomplishment, Gotama is described as incomparable, supreme (*anuttara*), and "victorious over all" (*sabbābhibhū*).[27] The *Visuddhimagga* detaches the adjective "supreme" (*anuttara*) from the combination "supreme charioteer of men to be tamed" (*anuttara purisadammasārathi*) and takes it as a distinct attribute denoting the Buddha's uniqueness. Peerless, he surpasses the whole world in wisdom and virtue and stands alone without a counterpart.[28]

Because of these descriptions of Gotama's wisdom, power and supremacy, people in ancient India asked – as people newly acquainted with the Buddhist tradition still ask today – was Gotama a god or a man? The question is a reasonable one since many of the qualities attributed to Gotama are like those attributed to deities in other religious traditions. According to the canonical texts, Gotama himself answered this question when it was posed by a brahman visitor. On that occasion, he said that he was neither a god nor a spirit nor even a human being any longer because he had overcome the mental states that constitute beings on those planes of existence; rather, he was a Buddha.[29] Other accounts explain that he was a "man in his last body,"[30] one who had become more than a man, who had become a fully-enlightened Buddha. The commentaries point out that this name, Buddha, is not a name given by a mother or a father but is a true description of Buddhas and Exalted Ones who have reached omniscient wisdom and liberation.[31] Gotama was believed to have become the "seventh sage,"[32] the seventh in the line of universal Buddhas. As such, he was clearly supreme in the world of gods and men, occupying a place similar to that of the ocean among waters or the sun among heavenly bodies.[33]

A contemporary Theravādin expresses the belief of generations of Buddhists when he writes, "The Buddha is revered not as a personality of such and such a name but as the embodiment of Enlightenment."[34] The tradition states that Gotama, like the Buddhas of previous ages, discovered the supramundane Dhamma.[35] Gotama said that he had discovered an ancient path taken by the Buddhas of former times.[36] After he reached enlightenment on his own, when pondering the matter of which teacher or ascetic he should then follow, Gotama realized that having surpassed all teachers, all gods and men, he could only follow Dhamma. So he lived under Dhamma.[37] Having fulfilled the paths, the fruitions, and Nibbāna, Gotama represented and manifested the transcendent Dhamma or the ultimate reality for the present age.

(4) One further group of attributes predicated of the Buddha relates to the qualities we have noted – spiritual perfection and his role as the supreme being for our world – but this group of attributes reveals more clearly the religious significance of the Buddha for his followers. These attributes pertain to his compassion for the world and his ability to offer a solution to the human predicament. Not only has a fully-enlightened Buddha arisen for our age, but his arising makes a difference. The *Visuddhimagga* explains that "wisdom and virtuous conduct" (*vijjācaraṇa*) denotes that union of the Buddha's omniscient wisdom and his great compassion (*mahā-karuṇā*).[38] Through his omniscience he knows the needs of all beings and through his compassion he aids them. In a well known passage from the canonical texts or *suttas*, the Buddha proclaims that he has arisen in the world out of compassion for beings and in order to bring about the welfare and happiness of gods and men.[39]

Two of the nine attributes in the salutation to the Buddha refer to his compassionate action on behalf of beings. He guides and tames persons the way a coachman tames his horses (*purisa-dammasārathi*). He is also called a "teacher of gods and men," a role which the commentary explains by playing on the term "teacher" (*satthar*) and comparing him to the leader of a caravan (*sattha*). Just as a caravan leader causes the caravan to cross the desert safely, so the Buddha brings people across the desert of existence to safety.[40]

A beautiful analogy given in the *suttas* summarizes all these attributes of the Buddha and expresses what one writer has called "the essential religious value of the Buddha for Buddhism."[41] Just as the world is in darkness before the sun and the moon have arisen or evolved in it, so the world is in spiritual darkness before a *Tathāgata* arises.[42] Gotama, as the fully-enlightened Buddha, is the light of the world. He is enlightened and able to cause others to reach enlightenment.[43]

When the commentarial tradition turns from explanations of the Buddha's authority as a refuge to explanations of what it means for a person to go for refuge in the Buddha, it enlarges upon these beliefs concerning Gotama's compassionate activity in the world. For those who go for refuge to him, the Buddha is "the slayer of evil" and "the provider of welfare."[44] He is a refuge, the tradition maintains, because he "kills people's fears" by promoting their benefit and preventing their harm.[45] These statements seem to depict the Buddha as something more than merely a shining example. According to the commentaries, the Buddha was somehow actively involved in providing a solution to the human predicament.

These statements lead us back, then, to the question raised at the outset: How does going for refuge in the Buddha solve the human predicament? Buddhists have understood refuge in the Buddha, as well as in the Dhamma and the Sangha, to be a power-filled act. Emphasizing the potency of the act of refuge, the commentarial tradition says that going for refuge "kills" (*hiṃsati*) the fear, the suffering (*dukkha*), and the defilements leading to unsatisfactory existences.[46] But Buddhaghosa cautions that the salvation promised here is not automatic. It is not just a matter of going to the Buddha, but of going to the Buddha *as* refuge.[47] That is, the mode of going, the intention of the one who goes for refuge, must be right.[48] Buddhaghosa says that the proper mode of going is illustrated in this statement:

> I go to the Buddha as "refuge," he is for me the highest ideal, the destroyer of evil, the provider of benefit, with this intention I go to him (*gacchati*), resort to him (*bhajati*), serve him (*sevati*), and honor him (*payirupāssati*), or thus I know (*janāti*), I understand (*bujjhati*).[49]

The mode of going is specified in this passage by the series of verbs beginning with "I go," *gacchati*, and ending with "I understand," *bujjhati*. Arranged as they are, these terms indicate a significant progression, a movement from going for refuge to attaining enlightenment. Buddhaghosa notes that the verbal roots meaning "going" also signify "knowing."[50] The inter-relation of these terms suggests that going for refuge involves one in a process of liberation, a process in which the end is implicit in the beginning. As John Ross Carter has written, by going for refuge "one is entering a process of transcending,"[51] a process of transforming one's outlook and one's life.

The commentarial tradition explains the function of refuge in this process of transcending by defining refuge in terms of the path (*magga*) with its mundane (*lokiya*) and supramundane (*lokuttara*) aspects (*KhpA.*, 17f.; *M.A.* I.132). On the mundane level, refuge provides not only an entrance to the path for the unenlightened, but also ways of moving toward the goal, as we learn from the commentarial explanation of the "four modes of going for refuge." The commentarial tradition contains at least two versions of these modes of refuge. One version appears in identical terms in the commentaries to the *Dīgha-Nikāya*, the *Majjhima-Nikāya*, and the *Aṅguttara-Nikāya*.[52] The other version is found in the commentary to the *Khuddaka-Pāṭha*.[53] Although very similar, these two versions have some interesting differences that seem to indicate two different streams of commentarial reflection on the *tisaraṇa*. According to the first group of commentaries the four modes or ways (*ākāra*) of going for refuge are (1) self-surrender or self-dedication (*attasanniyyātana*); (2) accepting the Buddha, the Dhamma, and the Sangha as one's highest ideal (*tapparāyanata*); (3) taking up the status of a pupil or disciple (*sissabhāvūpagamana*); and (4) prostrating oneself (*paṇipāta*).[54] In the *Paramatthajotikā I* (*KhpA.*) the four modes are listed as (1) resolution (*samādāna*), (2) taking up the status of a pupil or disciple (*sissabhāvūpagamana*), (3) leading to the goal (*tapponatta*), and (4) self-surrender or self-dedication (*attasanniyyātana*). From the titles of the modes and from the explanations and illustrations given for them in the commentaries, we see that three of the four modes in these two versions are virtually identical: modes 2, 3, and 4 in *KhpA.* parallel modes 3, 2, and 1 in *MA*. The order in which the modes are given seems to be traditional and, perhaps, significant. Although listed in inverse order, the three parallel modes stand in the same relation to each other. The other mode, different in the two versions, is placed at the beginning/end of the series rather than in-between any of the three parallel modes. A list of the Pāli titles of the modes shows these similarities.

KhpA.	*MA.*
1. *samādāna*	4. *panipāta*
2. *sissabhāvūpagamana*	3. *sissabhāvūpagamana*
3. *tapponatta*	2. *tapparāyanata*
4. *attasanniyyātana*	1. *attasanniyyātana*

The Venerable Nyanaponika suggests that these modes represent definite stages of devotion "given [in *MA.* and parallels] in what seems to be a descending order beginning from the highest form, the complete self-surrender, and ending with the lowest, the Homage by Prostration."[55] In his article, Nyanaponika speculates that these modes once were regarded as formulas and taken as vows by devotees. Those who took these vows hoped to progress from the lower vows and stages to the higher by eliminating their defilements at each stage just as in fulfilling the *jhānas* or stages of concentration.

Ven. Nyanaponika's explanation is intriguing and accounts for some important aspects of the modes, specifically their serial order and the solemn phrase repeated after the modes, "Thus may you know me."[56] Although we cannot rule out the possibility that these modes were once administered as vows and seen as stages of devotion, the commentarial accounts do not quite seem to support this interpretation. The commentaries refer to these modes as "various ways" and say that any one of the four modes constitutes a valid "going for refuge."[57]

Without regarding these modes as distinct stages, we can, nevertheless, take them as illustrating the essential dynamic or intention involved in going for refuge. The modes show that one who goes for refuge should undertake to live as a disciple of the Buddha following the pattern of either the first lay disciples, Tappassu and Bhallika, or the great elder Mahā-Kassapa, who inherited the Buddha's robes.[58] More than this, true refuge requires that one make the Buddha, the Dhamma, and the Sangha one's highest ideals, *parāyana*. Nyanaponika notes that in this context the term *parāyana* means "Guiding Ideal" or "the Way to the Beyond."[59] Re-orienting one's life to this ideal demands a sacrifice such as was made by the brahman Brahmāyu[60] who, in order to follow the Buddha, cast aside his own considerable reputation and status as a master of the *Vedas*. Even beyond this sacrifice, however, refuge finally involves total surrender of the self. Nyanaponika is surely correct that self-surrender, *attasanniyyatāna*, represents the highest mode of devotion.[61] The modes of refuge in the commentaries culminate in this act of dedicating oneself completely to the Buddha as the guiding ideal. In order to take refuge in the Buddha, one must relinquish the false refuge of the ego. The commentarial analysis of the modes of going for refuge thus depicts a profound process of shifting the center of one's existence away from the self and to the triple gem.

As a way of summarizing these mundane modes of going for refuge, the commentaries say that refuge amounts to the attainment of faith, *saddhā*.[62] *Saddhā*, or faith, in this context means recognizing in the Buddha, the Dhamma, and the Sangha a more ultimate level of reality that transcends one's ego and deciding to orient one's life to that reality (*parāyana*). For Buddhists, this faith is not the solution to the human predicament, but understood as the subordination of ego; *saddhā* — and the refuge process — relates directly to the solution to the human predicament. Buddhists describe this predicament as *dukkha*, "suffering" or the "unsatisfactoriness" of existence. The cause of this suffering is ignorance or wrong perception of reality. As Donald Swearer has written, "Life is suffering because we are trying to live on a level of reality which does not exist."[63] Basic to this misperception of reality is the ego-illusion, our belief that our self or ego constitutes the absolute and pivotal reality. This illusion produces suffering because we inevitably find that the world neither responds nor corresponds to our egocentric desires and will. To solve this predicament of ego/ignorance/suffering, Buddhists have said one must develop wisdom, replacing wrong perceptions of self and world with the true perception. And the way to this truth lies through insight meditation which develops our awareness of reality until we clearly and intuitively see the process nature of existence, marked by "no-self" or "egolessness" (*anatta*), "impermanence (*anicca*), and "suffering" or "unsatisfactoriness" (*dukkha*). Meditation is a much-debated and many-faceted phenomenon, but Swearer accurately described the Buddhist understanding of the function of meditation when he wrote, "Exercises in meditation simply provide the context in which such understanding [of the way things really are, *i.e.*, of *anicca*, *anatta* and *dukkha*] can be developed and nurtured."[64]

If meditation is the context for developing this wisdom, faith, or *saddhā*, and refuge serve as the antecedent context for meditation and wisdom. For although full realization of this truth through insight lies far from the ordinary person who is mired in ignorance, the commentaries show that progress toward the truth of *anatta* begins when one subordinates the ego by means of the refuges. A person who attains *saddhā* as the modes of refuge specify can set about living the truth of *anatta* through wisdom. This is a necessary step because as long as people live by asserting their egos they will never be able to grasp the truth of egolessness. This conception of the process of gaining wisdom reflects the Buddhists' belief that the wisdom they seek to gain is not detached from life. Saving wisdom relates to life and must be lived. The truth of egolessness (*anatta*), central to the wisdom that liberates beings from their predicament, has thus been regarded as not merely an ontological truth, but, perhaps primarily, as an ethical or existential truth indicating a way of living that brings authentic existence. As one scholar has observed, for Theravāda Buddhists "the fundamental concern in *anatta* doctrine is not so much with its metaphysical truth – though this too is asserted with great confidence – as its experiential religious value."[65]

If going for refuge thus marks the beginning of the path to wisdom, the commentaries show by the same logic that refuge also continues to play a part on the supramundane level of the path. The *Paramatthajotikā I* (*KhpA.*) posits as a fifth mode of going for refuge – higher than the mode of self-surrender – going for refuge of the noble person (*ariyapuggala*) who, having cut off the defilements, has entered the path to Nibbāna.[66] The *Majjhima-Nikāya Aṭṭhakathā* (*MA.*) says that on the supramundane level those noble persons who have entered the path practice going for refuge with Nibbāna as their object.[67] Going for refuge bears fruit, the commentaries say, on both the mundane and supramundane levels.[68] On the mundane level, those who go for refuge attain not only faith but also pleasant lives and favorable rebirths;[69] whereas, those who go for refuge on the supramundane level achieve the supreme goal: wisdom and the cessation of *dukkha*.[70] To be sure, the commentarial tradition does not maintain here that refuge or *saddhā* alone accomplishes the goal, but it does assert that going for refuge is a powerful act effective and necessary even at the highest stages of the path to wisdom.

Since refuge in the Buddha leads to salvation by enabling a person to enter and continue in the process of transcending, then what answer should we give to the second question raised at the outset: Did the Buddha liberate beings or teach that each being must strive for its own individual salvation? Our analysis of the meaning of refuge in the Buddha indicates that both the Buddha and individual salvation-striving are necessary to attain the goal of liberation.

The commentarial explanation of refuge bears out the traditional Buddhist emphasis on striving. There can be no doubt that the Buddhist tradition has stressed individual striving in reference to both the means and the end of salvation. Regarding the means, the texts state that the Buddha only indicates the way to liberation and individuals must strive to actualize this way. In the *Dhammapada* we read, "You yourselves must exert effort (*ātappaṃ*). The *Tathāgatas* only show the way."[71] Likewise, in the *suttas*, the Buddha explains that he only points the way to Nibbāna; he can no more guarantee that his disciples will reach it than one who gives a traveller directions for reaching a distant city can guarantee that the traveller will follow the directions properly and arrive at the destination.[72] Although the Buddha had great compassion for the plight of humanity he could not effect human salvation automatically. Throughout his teachings, the Buddha seems to have stressed the necessity of knowing and seeing the truth for oneself. He compared the brahmans to a line of blind men each holding on to the one before because none of the teachers in their lineage could claim that he personally had known and seen the truth.[73] According to Buddhists, nothing less than personal realization (knowing and seeing) of the truth can counteract the ignorance binding us to *saṃsāra*. For this reason, the Buddha, nearing the end of his life, admonished his disciples, "Dwell making yourself your island, yourself your refuge; do not dwell with any other refuge. Dwell making the Dhamma your island, the Dhamma your refuge; do not dwell with any other refuge."[74] This is the supreme teaching about refuge. It declares that a person must finally go beyond refuge in the Buddha and take refuge in the supreme Dhamma.

Going for refuge to the Buddha thus does not contradict the necessity for individual striving. Although refuge leads to faith (*saddhā*), it is not a salvation by faith alone. The commentarial division of refuge into mundane and supramundane aspects indicates that refuge, traditionally, was regarded as ancillary to the path rather than as a separate path in itself. The function of refuge in the Theravāda religious system seems equivalent to the explanation of the function of faith given in the *Kītāgirisutta* (*M.* I. 479f.):

> O Monks, one who has faith approaches [the teacher], approaching he sits down near by, sitting near by he lends an attentive ear, lending ear he hears the Dhamma, having heard the Dhamma, he bears it in mind ... having weighed and examined it he strives, striving he realizes the ultimate truth, and having penetrated it by wisdom he sees.

But although the commentarial explanations of refuge in the Buddha do not diminish the importance of individual effort, these explanations of refuge coupled with the prominence in Theravāda practice of the ritual of the threefold refuge indicate that we must clarify what it means to say that Theravāda is a tradition of individual salvation-striving. The refuges seem to point to several important qualifications of this individual salvation-striving stereotype. First, for all persons except the rare *Paccekabuddhas*, whose path does not constitute a realistic option for the masses, the Buddha represents an essential component of the path to liberation. If the tradition has maintained that the Buddhas only point the way to the goal, it has also held that only the Buddhas point the way to the goal. Individuals must strive for their own salvation, but without the Buddha this striving would be aimless and fruitless. Refuge represents the necessary complement to individual striving, for as the *Dhammapada* teaches, those who do not know the Buddha, the Dhamma, and the Sangha seek refuge in caves and forests and shrines, but these refuges do not lead to safety or to liberation. By taking refuge in the Buddha, the Dhamma, and the Sangha, however, one can attain the "safe refuge," the supreme wisdom and liberation.[75] In the *Kītāgirisutta*, cited above, we noted that one must develop faith to progress on the path, but that *sutta* also says that if one did not encounter the *Tathāgata* and then "draw close" with faith, no progress would be made on the path. Both individual faith (striving) and the Buddha as the proper object of that faith are necessary.

With the doctrine of the Truly Enlightened One (*sammāsambuddha*), Buddhists have proclaimed that the Buddha's existence was not incidental to human liberation. Gotama arose in this world as the Buddha for our age, the one who made the Dhamma known where it would not have been known otherwise. For all but a minute percentage of humanity capable of discovering the Dhamma without a guide, the Buddha was the only hope for liberation, the one who "opened the doors to deathlessness."[76] It is not just as a teacher of the Dhamma, however, that the Buddha had significance for salvation. The tradition declares that Gotama lived the Dhamma; he embodied the salvation ideal. As Wilfred Cantwell Smith has observed, the marvelous legends about the birth, enlightenment, and death of the Buddha represent the traditional Buddhist belief that "the whole universe was astir in the process of the Dharma's being made known to mankind."[77]

Second, just as we must say that individual effort apart from the Buddha's guidance is insufficient as a means to salvation, so we should note also that the goal of salvation has an extra-individual character. In the end, although we must see the truth and attain Nibbāna for ourselves, we do not create the possibility of our salvation. The Dhamma that individuals must make their supreme refuge exists prior to individual realization of it. By finding the Dhamma we do not find a private salvation, but, rather, we find the salvific possibility inherent in existence. The Dhamma represents, Smith has written, "an ultimately real, a final truth in accordance with which if a man lives he will be saved."[78] John Ross Carter has referred to Dhamma as "salvific Truth" and has said "*Dhamma*, salvific Truth, abides and is not remote from persons." — "One of the oldest and most frequent glosses . . . for the term *'dhamma* has been *'dhāretī ti dhammo'* – *dhamma* is so called because it holds, supports.'"[79] The Dhamma is the "good news" that the Buddha discovered and re-presented; because the Dhamma prevails, because "there is such a thing as Nibbāna,"[80] individuals can attain liberation.[81] For, as Smith says, "If there were no eternal Dharma, then man could not possibly save himself."[82] Refuge in the Buddha opens the way to attaining the ultimate refuge of the Dhamma.

Finally, then, the relation of refuge to the goal of liberation suggests a fundamental philosophical qualification of the notion of "individual salvation-striving": although individuals must strive, in the end salvation or liberation in the Buddhist tradition is not individualistic. According to the Buddhist tradition, in ultimate truth existence is characterized by no-self, *anatta*. Refuge, thus, serves as a skillful means (*upāya*) of orienting persons to ultimate truth. The person who goes for refuge in the Buddha by making the effort himself, by committing himself to the Buddha, finally attains the realization of the absence of self. Thus, from the perspective of ultimate truth or the Dhamma, the Buddhist tradition represents not a "radical form of individual salvation-striving" but rather a radical form of non-individual salvation.

Conclusion

In sum, salvation in the Theravāda tradition turns out to be not as ruggedly individual as it has sometimes been portrayed. The emphasis on individual effort and striving represents only one side of the salvation process. Buddha, the Dhamma, and the Sangha represent the other side of this process and the act of going for refuge functions as a way of balancing the two sides of the dialectic of salvation. For this reason, Theravāda Buddhists have traditionally believed and taught that going for refuge to the Buddha enables one to enter the way leading to the solution to the human predicament.

This view of the Buddha as refuge has significance for our understanding of the Theravāda Buddhist tradition as a whole for it indicates the essential role of devotion. The devotional element represented by the refuges does not stand isolated from the primary path to liberation. The refuges, often classed as a part of a "lower path" of devotion intended primarily for the laity, actually cannot be separated from the true path itself. The tradition has integrity; devotional practices, rightly understood, participate in the central meaning and intention of the tradition. Going for refuge in the Buddha does not constitute salvation or even, by itself, a sufficient means to salvation, but it does contribute in an essential way to the development of salvific wisdom. As a Sinhalese Theravāda Buddhist has written, "Devotion is an indispensable aid on the way to deliverance."[83]

3 Dhamma as Refuge
in the Theravāda Buddhist Tradition[1]

John Ross Carter

A LITTLE MORE than a century ago, a Wesleyan catechist, F. S. Sirimanne, took issue with some Buddhist *bhikkhus* in a debate held in Pānadura, Sri Lanka. Turning to the notion of Dhamma in the threefold refuge (*tisaraṇa*), Mr. Sirimanne said,

> What refuge is there for you from Dharma? Dharma means books written on *ola* leaves. How can those books be support for you? Is it not that those books exist by your 'refuge' [*saraṇa*].[2]

The Pānadura debate and others occurring in Sri Lanka at about the same time represent a low mark in attempts to understand the faith and tradition of men and women participating in the Buddhist and Christian traditions in Sri Lanka. One hardly thinks Mr.Sirimanne's comments were sincere, certainly the comments represent a position that was ill-informed; also, for that matter, the same appears to have been the case with some challenges posed by the *bhikkhus* involved in that debate.

But Mr. Sirimanne's remarks serve as a rationale for this brief essay: for some, the meaning of Dhamma in the threefold refuge might not be entirely clear. Certainly the meaning seems to have escaped Mr. Sirimanne's understanding, and scholars since have not been altogether precise when discussing the meaning of Dhamma in the *tisaraṇa*, hence creating a tendency, inadvertently perhaps, among readers to fail to grasp the full import of the weighty notion of Dhamma as refuge.

On numerous occasions scholars of the Theravāda Buddhist tradition have been somewhat misleading in their presentation of the notion of Dhamma in the threefold refuge (*tisaraṇa*). I say "misleading" because I would not wish to pose as one imputing misunderstanding of the notion of Dhamma on the part of numerous scholars. I choose to speak of their work as misleading for a reader who might not have had the good fortune of studying Buddha-dhamma as closely as have these scholars and consequently might not have recourse to their scholarly understanding of the Buddhist tradition.

Some scholars have translated *Dhamma* in the threefold refuge as "Law"[3] or "Teaching,"[4] or "Doctrine,"[5] and some have noted that Dhamma in this context designates the preaching of the Buddha now recorded in the scriptures.[6] One might say these interpretations are, on the whole, acceptable. My concern in this chapter is to demonstrate that these interpretations are not adequate and a representative list of authors, writing in different centuries or decades, writing from different perspectives with different purposes, would be illustrative of the ease with which a reader might be misled.[7]

These interpretations of Dhamma as refuge are not wrong; they are misleading because they are inadequate.

What then is the meaning of Dhamma in the threefold refuge? What would be a more adequate interpretation? In response to Mr. Sirimanne's remarks at Pānadura, Ven. Guṇānanda Thera, an orator of note at that time, replied,

> What is said by going for refuge in Dharma is not going for refuge in scriptural (*baṇa*) books. The noble gem of the ninefold Saddharma that transcends the world preached by the Buddha is called Dharma. That Dharma is the teacher even of the Buddha. If a person were to believe that Dharma and practice according to it, he would obtain deliverance in the next world. The idea of going for refuge in Dharma should be understood in this way.[8]

Debates tend to move at a rather quick pace, but Ven. Guṇānanda, standing before the crowd assembled at Pānadura, pointed in the direction in which this chapter will move. One notes that Ven. Guṇānanda indicated an important distinction between the books that Mr. Sirimanne saw, the books made from *ola* leaves, and the books that he saw, scripture, *baṇa* books, in which are recorded the teaching of the Buddha. Yet, Ven. Guṇānanda did not stress this distinction nor did he dwell on another: between recorded scripture and the teaching itself with which one is to become engaged, known as *pariyatti-dhamma*, Dhamma that is to be thoroughly learned, the authoritative teaching, authoritative norm. Nevertheless, Ven. Guṇānanda, on August 28, 1873, when he mentioned the ninefold Dhamma that transcends the world as Dhamma to which one goes for refuge, represented well a tradition at least one thousand and five hundred years old.[9] And this tradition has continued into recent times in Sri Lanka.[10]

Precisely what Dhamma meant when the Buddha first spoke it is now, it appears, beyond our grasp through historical inquiry on the basis of materials at hand. The word has an unusually broad field of reference, a broad spectrum of meaning, undergoing a fluid shifting of nuance in differing contexts in which it was used. In its broadest sense, Dhamma referred to that which the Buddha said and also to that which he discovered.

In the early phase of the Buddhist movement, persons expressed publicly a personal reorientation of life, in life, to life, by taking refuge in the Buddha as one who possessed those qualities that evoke adoration from others (*Bhagavan*) and also in Dhamma, the words of the Buddha, the way of the Buddha, and that to which the words referred, to which the way led. However, rather soon in the early phase of the Buddhist movement, a threefold formula (Buddha, Dhamma, Sangha (*sāvakasaṅgha*)) became standard.[11]

Regarding Dhamma in this context of refuge, the commentaries tell us,

> Dhamma is used in the sense that it supports [*dhāreti*] those who have attained the path, who have realized cessation [*sacchikatanirodha*], who are following along accordingly, who are not falling into the four hells.[12]

One notes that the first move in the commentarial tradition is to provide some explanation for the occurrence of the word *Dhamma*. The attempts of the Pāli commentators of old to provide an etymological derivation for a term have frequently been criticized, if not ridiculed, by brilliant Western philologists, and more recently by some Sinhalese Buddhists trained in the scientific method of philology. Of course the methods of the commentators were often lacking in philological exactitude. However, the commentators were remarkable in communicating homiletical plenitude when working with or squeezing (for philologists, forcing) seemingly possible etymological derivations of the Pāli terms.[13] In the case of the term *Dhamma*, it is derived from the root *dhṛ*, "to hold, to bear, to support" and the commentators thus far are on the mark. But they introduce the reader to something new; an insight into a soteriological process — Dhamma refers to that which enables a person who becomes engaged with it not to fall.

And the tradition has long remembered this point, profound in its soteriological ramifications. One commentary reads,

> Dhamma is used [as a term (symbol?)] because it upholds. Because it does not allow one to fall is what is meant.[14]

In another commentary, there is the following:

> Dhamma is used in the sense of upholding those following along accordingly from falling into the suffering of the hells.[15]

And elsewhere, one reads,

> "Dhamma" — because of the upholding of those who have cultivated the way and those who have realized Nibbāna in the sense that there is no falling into hells. . . .[16]

And another text adds, "without deviation [*nippariyāyena*]";[17]still another text speaks more generally of an upholding "from a fall into the suffering of *saṃsāra*."[18] And a Sinhalese text picks this up nicely by drawing attention to

> . . . Dharma that leads on, which is called Dharma because it upholds beings who are upholding it without allowing them to fall into the four hells and *saṃsāra*.[19]

One is met, therefore, in the commentarial tradition, firstly with a profound religious affirmation about Dhamma to which one goes for refuge — it supports, keeps one from falling. This affirmation provides the context into which the further discussions of Dhamma in the threefold refuge are placed. In the final analysis neither the Buddha nor the eight noble persons constituting the *sāvakasaṅgha*[20] can provide this support. It is Dhamma alone that supports the one engaged with it.

Now, what is Dhamma that supports, keeps one from falling, to which one goes for refuge? We are told, "In effect, it [Dhamma] is both the noble way and Nibbāna."[21] And, further, it is pointed out,

> Not only [is Dhamma] both the noble way and also Nibbāna but also is Dhamma [taken as] authoritative norm or teaching [*pariyattidhamma*] together with the noble fruits.[22]

Dhamma is the way and also Nibbāna together with the authoritative norm or teaching. One must admit that this is a rather comprehensive interpretation of Dhamma, but the tradition has not been put off, as it were, by this. Manifestly have Buddhists held to it, perhaps because they have recognized that they have been held by it.

Quite early, and one can never be entirely certain about these things, the elders, *theras*, chose to remember a verse that has played a significant role in the forming of attitudes of Buddhists about Dhamma in the threefold refuge; a verse occurring in the canonical strata, quoted in the commentaries and memorized by Sinhalese Buddhist school children today. Some who have lived and worked in Sri Lanka might have heard these school children reciting a form of the threefold refuge (*tisaraṇa*) formula almost at the top of their voices, or so it seemed — a sound wafting noticeably over the paddy fields or forming a part of the hubbub at a busy intersection — as they would recite the second stanza of the formula, the verse dealing with Dhamma:

Rāgavirāgam anejam asokaṃ
Dhammam asaṃkhatam appaṭikūlaṃ
Madhuram imaṃ paguṇam suvibhattaṃ
Dhammam imaṃ saraṇatthaṃ upemi.[23]

Perhaps the children were oblivious to the force of the words they recited but a passer-by is witness, at least, to an attempt, however fraught with human foibles, to pass along to a new generation the ideal aspirations of an old tradition.

Let me proffer this translation:

I go for refuge to this sweet, learned,
well apportioned Dhamma;
Free from lust of passion, without turmoil,
without sorrow,
Dhamma not conditioned, without disgust.

This relatively late, but nevertheless canonical, verse suggests that we are touching upon a religious apprehension that our English words "Law" or "Doctrine" or "Teaching" fail to reflect. The *theras* who chose to remember this verse, the commentarial tradition that utilized it, and the school children who have chanted it have all placed it in a context dealing with the notion of taking refuge in Dhamma.

This verse has embedded in it the comprehensive interpretation of Dhamma as refuge, which Buddhaghosa, in the fifth century A.D., passed along to posterity when he recorded a commentarial interpretation of Dhamma as follows:

> Here [in this verse] 'free from lust of passion' means the way [or path, *magga*,] that is described. 'Without turmoil, without sorrow' is the fruit. 'Dhamma that is not conditioned' is Nibbāna. 'Without disgust, sweet, learned, well apportioned' means the collections of Dhamma divided into the three *piṭakas*.[24]

Of course, the commentarial tradition is considered rather late from the point of view of one interested solely in determining what might have been the interpretations espoused by Buddhists in the early phases of the Buddhist movement. However, the commentarial tradition is early from the perspective of one attempting to understand the way a tradition has maintained continuity for roughly fifteen hundred years.

Dhammapāla, who flourished apparently not long after Buddhaghosa, elaborates a bit more in his commentary on this verse, but follows closely the guidelines of his notable predecessor. "By 'free from lust of passion'," Dhammapāla tells us,[25]

> is meant the noble path. By means of this the noble ones detach themselves from passions developed from time immemorial. "Without turmoil, without sorrow," means the noble fruit, which is designated as without turmoil, without sorrow because of the total pacification of the traces of craving considered to be turmoil and of the defilements associated with sorrow. "Dhamma" is Dhamma having its own inherent nature [*sabhāvadhamma*]. Indeed, Dhamma to be grasped because of its own inherent nature is the path, fruit, and Nibbāna and not in the sense of ratiocinative characteristics [*paññatti*] like the textual Dhamma.[26] And also, the term "Dhamma" means Dhamma in the highest sense, that is, Nibbāna.

Dhammapāla, following the older tradition, agrees that "sweet," "learned," and "well apportioned" have to do with the authoritative norm of teaching, the textual Dhamma (*pariyatti-dhamma*).

We have before us at this point a traditional Theravāda interpretation of Dhamma as path, as fruit, and as Nibbāna, with a recognition of Dhamma that is to be thoroughly learned, mastered, *i.e.*, the authoritative norm, the authoritative teaching, textual Dhamma.

The Theravāda tradition has made much of the notion of path, fruit, and Nibbāna, refining it in the sense of four paths, four fruits, and Nibbāna, and speaking of this interpretation as the "nine-fold world transcending Dhamma," or *navavidhalokuttara-dhamma.*

We have, then, Dhamma understood on the one hand as authoritative teaching (*pariyatti-dhamma*) and on the other hand as a soteriological process, *i.e.*, paths, fruits, and Nibbāna. This is elaborated by Buddhaghosa in the seventh chapter of his *Visuddhimagga,* and has been held consistently within the Sinhalese Theravāda tradition.

It is crucial to have a clear understanding of these two dimensions of Dhamma in the threefold refuge. The nine-fold world transcending Dhamma is that about which the authoritative teaching speaks. Although the authoritative teaching is to be learned and kept in mind, it is the nine-fold world transcending Dhamma that is to be attained, realized (*paṭivedha*). This nine-fold world transcending Dhamma comprises the path of "stream attainment" (*sotāpatti*) and its fructification or fruit (*phala*), the path of a "once returner" (*sakadāgāmin*) and its fruit, the path of a "non-returner" (*anāgāmin*) and its fruit, the path of the state of an *arahant* and its fruit, and, as the ninth factor, Nibbāna. And one who attains the first path, a "stream-attainer," is assured of attaining Nibbāna because of the regularity of Dhamma.[27]

We are told,

> More noble the fruit of stream attainment
> Than an empire on the earth,
> Than going to heaven,
> Than sovereignty over the whole world.[28]

Dhamma supports; one is to learn thoroughly the authoritative teaching (*pariyatti-dhamma*) now preserved in books (*pāḷi-dhamma*), if no longer held in mind. Seeking refuge in *pariyatti-dhamma,* not the books themselves, is part of what is meant by Dhamma to which one goes for refuge. But there is more than this, much more. Dhamma as refuge is also the nine-fold Dhamma that transcends the world(s), it is the soteriological process on the highest level, in the highest sense, Dhamma that can be penetrated (*paṭivedha*).

How then might one translate *Dhamma* in the phrase ("I go to Dhamma as refuge")? "Law," "Teaching," "Doctrine" will not do. Perhaps, a more adequate translation is "salvific Truth,"[29] using the adjective "salvific" to remind us of this quality of truth. Truth, when known, is freeing, liberating. And "salvific Truth" represents well the understanding of Theravāda Buddhists who have long known salvific Truth which is the teaching of the Buddha (*pariyatti-dhamma*), salvific Truth which can be lived (*paṭipatti-dhamma*), and salvific Truth which can be attained (*adhigama*), realized (*paṭivedha-dhamma*).[30]

4 The Sangha as Refuge
in the Theravāda Buddhist Tradition[1]

Edmund F. Perry and Shanta Ratnayaka

IN RECITING the threefold refuge (*tisaraṇa*), Buddhist monks as well as Buddhist layfolk verbally express the highest veneration for the three gems (*tiratana*): The Buddha, the dhamma and the sangha. To what do they refer when they say, "I take refuge in the sangha" (*Saṅghaṃ saraṇaṃ gacchāmi*)? Do these Buddhist monks and lay persons actually revere what people generally identify as the sangha, namely, the order or community of yellow-robed monks? Or does the sangha of the *tiratana* refer rather to a different order, and if so, do householders and monastics have the same or a different relation to it?

The marked contrast in daily routine of Theravāda householders and Theravāda monks has no bearing on their relations to the sangha of the triple gem. The conspicuous conventional distinction between layfolk and monks ought not to obscure the Buddha's teaching that the laity and monks attain beatitude by the same means. The path to perfection consists of something other than the differences between the life-style of the householder and the monastic. To discern the proper relation of both layperson and monk to the path requires Buddhists and scholars of the Buddhist tradition to return to and probe carefully the Buddha's own words.

The point we want to make in this chapter is that the householder's life is not a second-rate way to perfection and we propose to do this by clarifying the identity of the sangha of the three gems, that sangha venerated by monk and layperson alike.

In examining this subject, we must note certain misunderstandings that have arisen with respect to ordination and the order of Buddhist monks. A widespread popular misconception identifies the sangha solely and completely with the society or organization of Buddhist monks. This misconception encourages the equally incorrect notion that in the Theravāda Buddhist tradition ordination carries with it some sanctifying powers, benefits and privileges which qualitatively distinguish the holiness of monks from the holiness of the laity. An accurate understanding of two distinct meanings and uses of *saṅgha* in Buddhist doctrine and tradition will move us beyond both misconceptions.

Even before the time of Gotama Buddha, the word *saṅgha* (literally meaning "herd" or "assembly") was used in India to designate a band of monastics. The Buddha's followers took and used it to refer to any group of ordained persons (*bhikkhus*) who had renounced the householder's life. In Buddhist texts the phrase *bhikkhusaṅgha* (monk-sangha) occurs frequently. The Buddha addressed many of his discourses to monks, opening the discourse typically with the vocative, "O Bhikkus, . . ." Similarly, we often encounter in these discourses and elsewhere the phrase *bhikkhusaṅgha*.

Indeed the texts themselves contain many instances of persons who, not adequately understanding, specifically stated *bhikkhusaṅgha* when taking the three refuges. The *Majjhimanikāya* recounts the story of Upāli who became a follower of the Buddha's teaching. Upāli, previously a disciple of Nigaṇṭha Nātaputta, came to the Buddha, listened to his teaching and became at once completely persuaded by the teaching. Thereupon he said to the Buddha, "Lord, I take refuge in the Blessed One, in the dhamma, and in the bhikkhusangha."[2] However, *bhikkhusaṅgha* clearly differs from *sāvakasaṅgha*, "disciple-sangha," which also appears in the same literature and which the Buddha himself designates as the sangha of the three refuges. The use of the two words and the respective attending explanations differ so conspicuously as to spare us from agonizing over such issues as, "What does the word mean in this context?" When the word *saṅgha* occurs alone and *sāvakasaṅgha* is intended, the text specifies unmistakably and immediately that special meaning of the word.

Unfortunately translations, interpretations, and conventional usage manifest something less than precision, resulting in a confusion of the two sanghas. Among present-day Buddhists, in ordinary usage and in public understanding, sangha designates only the order of monks, the institutional society of ordained persons. Similarly, *sāvakasaṅgha* has escaped the common understanding of numerous monks as well as laypersons even in Buddhist countries. It should not surprise us, therefore, that the significant difference between the two sanghas has received little attention in Western scholarship.

The use of *saṅgha* to designate the society of Buddhist monks did not breach the conventional Indian meaning of the word. But the Buddha and his tradition innovated a very special and distinctive doctrinal meaning for "sangha." In this meaning the sangha consists of a community of disciples who have reached such sublime degrees of perfection and who live in such accord with the law of deliverance (the dhamma) that they cannot fail to go on to perfection.

This *sāvakasaṅgha* or community of noble persons (*ariyapuggala*) who cannot fall away from their exalted spiritual attainments[3] constituted a new idea in Indian religious thought. This special Buddhist meaning of sangha transcends the distinctions of lay and ordained persons. It includes persons who reached their sublime state through lay life and persons who became sublime through monastic life. *Sāvakasaṅgha*, disciple-sangha, as used in the Buddha's teaching, refers unquestionably to those noble persons (*ariyapuggala*) who have attained one or another of the eight blessed spiritual states on the path to full enlightenment.

The texts speak of these eight blessed ones as the "four pairs," since at each of four stages or paths (*magga*) a person realizes the stage itself and advances to realization of the fruit (*-phala*) of that stage. The individual who reaches a stage becomes a different individual when he completes that stage, thereby reaping the benefits of completing it. We can characterize the eight different kinds of spiritual individual in the *sāvakasaṅgha* as follows:

1. The holy one who, having entered the path of stream winning (*sotāpattimagga*), becomes free to disengage from the three

fetters of ego-belief, skeptical doubt, and attachment to rule and ritual;

2. The holy one who, having realized the fruit of winning the stream (*sotāpattiphala*), becomes freed from the first three fetters;

3. The holy one who, having realized the path of the once-returner (*sakadāgāmimagga*), freed from the first three fetters, becomes free to diminish the two additional fetters of sensuous craving and ill-will;

4. The holy one who, having realized the fruit of the path of the once-returner (*sakadāgāmiphala*), has become nearly freed of the fourth and fifth fetters;

5. The holy one who, having realized the path of the never-returner (*anāgāmimagga*), becomes free to disengage entirely from the five aforementioned fetters;

6. The holy one who, having realized the fruit of the never-returner (*anāgāmiphala*), has become completely freed from the first five fetters;

7. The holy one who,having realized the path of perfection (*arahattamagga*), begins to become freed from the five additional fetters of craving for rebirth in refined material existence, craving for immaterial existence, conceit, restlessness and ignorance;

8. The holy one who, having realized the fruit of perfection (*arahattaphala*), has become totally freed from all ten fetters.

These holy ones who make up the *sāvakasaṅgha* may have achieved their exalted status either as male or female householders or as male or female ascetics as we will show below. The sangha of the triple gem, the sangha venerated by lay and monastic Buddhists alike, is this *sāvakasaṅgha* of the Buddha's teaching. Both monks and laypeople "take refuge" in the triple gem; when saying "I take refuge in the sangha," either should mean, according to strict teaching, "I take refuge in these holy ones who, whether as householders or as ordained ascetics, male or female, have reached a point and path of holiness from which they cannot stray and which will inevitably lead them to total emancipation and enlightenment." Such holy ones, be they male or female, ordained or unordained, have reached a state of perfection from which they cannot fall, merit the reverence of others who would also go on to perfection.

A few examples will suffice to document this special meaning of sangha, identifying its membership with the eight (four pairs of) holy ones. In the *Aṅguttara-nikāya*[4] the Buddha instructs Visākha to purify the mind by meditating on the sangha. In the words of this instruction, one cannot possibly confuse the order of clergy with the subject proposed for meditation. The Buddha says:

> Visākha, the cleansing of the impure mind is accomplished by an appropriate procedure. How is this accomplished?
>
> The *aryan*-disciple calls to mind the sangha in this manner: The Blessed One's disciple-sangha (*sāvakasaṅgha*) is well-conducted, conducted uprightly, conducted in order, conducted properly ... they (the sangha) are the four pairs of beings, the eight persons [*aṭṭhapurisapuggala*] (refers to persons without distinction of laymen or monks). — The Blessed One's disciple-sangha is worthy of respect, offerings and gifts, worthy of being saluted with clasped hands, a field of merit unsurpassed for the whole world.
>
> As the *aryan*-disciple calls to mind the sangha, his mind is calmed, delight arises, the impurities of the mind are abandoned, just like the cleansing of a filthy garment by an appropriate washing procedure.

The commentary on this passage from the *Anguttara-nikāya* emphasizes that the Buddha intends the specific and special meaning of sangha here. In the commentary the crucial part reads in this way: "The Blessed One's disciple-sangha — that is, the four pairs of beings, the eight persons — is worthy of offering, oblations, gifts, and reverential salutation. It is a peerless field of merit for the world."

Again, the Ratanasutta of the *Sutta-nipāta* includes this statement:

> The eight persons, the four pairs who are the Buddha's disciples, are worthy of offerings. What is given to these will bear fruit. This precious gem inheres in the sangha, and by this truth may there be perfect happiness.[5]

Clearly, then, the doctrinal sangha, worthy of offerings, of reverence, of refuge, differs unmistakably from the society of yellow-robed, ordained monks. These scripture references make no mention of ordination as a prerequisite for becoming one of the eight holy ones in the Buddha's disciple-sangha. Buddhist scriptures record numerous and impressive examples of householders who achieved this blessed status, singling out both men and women as having realized the sublime states. In the *Saṃyutta-nikāya* the Buddha, replying to Ānanda, makes the following revealing remarks:

> Ānanda, the lay male disciple(*upāsaka*), named Sudatta has made an end by destroying the first three fetters and by weakening those of lust, hatred, and delusion, is a once-returner (*sakadāgāmi*): coming back to this world just once more he will make an end of *dukkha*.
>
> Sujātā, the lay woman disciple (*upāsikā*) who has made an end by destroying the first three fetters, is a stream-winner (*sotāpannā*), not doomed to lose her achievement, assured, bound for enlightenment.[6]

At the close of this same passage, the Buddha chides Ānanda for inquiring about so many different cases, whether this person or that person had become a holy one. He says:

> Ānanda, there were at Ñātika five hundred and six lay disciples who died and who, having destroyed three fetters, are stream-enterers (*sotāpannā*) not doomed to lose their realization, assured, destined for enlightenment.
>
> It is not surprising, Ānanda, that a human being dies. But if, when each one dies, you come and ask me about his realization, it is troublesome to the *Tathāgata*.[7]

Such passages from the canonical texts show that the dhamma of deliverance (enlightenment) deals no favoritism to monks and no discrimination against layfolk. Irrespective of householder or monastic status, the dhamma requires disciplined mental purification. From the passages just cited, it becomes evident that the Buddha himself recognized in many lay persons a state of mental purity, a holiness of mind, worthy of inclusion in his disciple-sangha.

One cannot adequately understand the meaning intended by the Buddhist use of the word *saṅgha* merely from references to dictionary etymologies or even from a good working knowledge of the canonical languages. The precise and proper meaning of *saṅgha* derives from Buddhist doctrine, from a correct understanding of the dhamma, the way, path, or law of purification and enlightenment realized and taught by the Buddha. A few passages from the canon itself will illustrate that the meaning of sangha derives from the fundamental teachings of the Buddha.

In the *Aṅguttara-nikāya*, on a certain occasion, the Buddha addresses Sāriputta and instructs him that a lay disciple can have the assurance that he has achieved the status of a stream winner ɜotāpanna). Indeed this passage asserts that the layperson can ·oth become a member of the *sāvakasaṅgha* and have present assurance that s/he has become a member of the *sāvakasaṅgha* ınd will not fall from that state — provided that the person find :ertain holy conditions within her- or himself. If "any white-rocked householder you know," the Buddha says to Sāriputta, is well-restrained in the five precepts, well-established in his veneration of the Buddha, the dhamma, and the sangha, endowed vith noble moral virtues, and unblemished, then such a person nay declare:

> For me hell is destroyed, animal rebirth is eliminated, the realm of ghosts is destroyed; destroyed for me also is the wayward way, the ill way, the abyss. I have entered the stream, not subject to any falling away, but assured and bound for enlightenment.[8]

The stream winner (well-restrained in the five precepts, well-established in his veneration of the Buddha, the dhamma, and the sangha, endowed with noble moral virtues, and unblemished) recognizes in himself the results of advanced knowledge of the Buddha's law of purification and deliverance, the results of disciplined observance of that law, and also the consequences of this knowledge and practice. The stream winner has all the evidence needed to be certain beyond doubt of belonging to that very sangha, the *sākavasaṅgha,* in which, as a stream winner, s/he holds unwavering faith.

Now consider how specifically the Buddha identifies the sangha of the noble disciples in the following passage where, again speaking to Sāriputta, he uses the words *saṅgha* and *sāvakasaṅgha,* synonymously. Note the italicized words in the Pali and compare them with our English translation which follows:

> *Puna ca param Sāriputta ariyasāvako* ***saṅghe*** *aveccappasādena samannāgato hoti supaṭipanno Bhagavato* ***sāvakasaṅgho****, ujupaṭipanno Bhagavato,* ***sāvakasaṅgho****.*[9]

In English translation this passage reads as follows:

> Again, Sāriputta, the noble disciple has unwavering faith in the *community*: well trained in the Exalted One's *community of disciples*; trained in uprightness is the Exalted One's *community of disciples.*

The above Pali quotation uses the word *saṅgha* first without an adjective, and then immediately in the same sentence repeats *saṅgha* several times with the adjective *sāvaka*. We quoted only a portion of the text, but that portion discloses two instances in which the Buddha used *sāvakasaṅgha* as a synonym of *saṅgha*. From the English translation, the reader can see how carefully the Buddha specified and clarified the meaning of words used in proclaiming the dhamma. One can also discern in this passage the inseparability of the various aspects of the Buddha's teaching. In the passage quoted, we should understand the community (*saṅgha*) or the community of disciples (*sāvakasaṅgha*) to include only those who have the particular spiritual achievements of "well trained," "trained in uprightness," and "unwavering faith in the community" of disciples. The stream-winner, and either of the other blessed ones, whether monk or lay disciple, gains unwavering faith in the disciple-sangha of the triple gem. This same passage, in lines we have not quoted, asserts that the disciple community has no other members than "the four pairs or the eight persons," which we discussed earlier. In the light of this evidence, we can consider an ordained monk (*bhikkhu*) a member of the disciple community only if he has attained one of the eight special spiritual stages.

What must we say further about the meaning and the status of the *bhikkhu*, the ordained monk?

We noted at the outset of this chapter that the word *bhikkhu* had currency in ancient India before the Buddha's time. In that ancient pre-Buddhist Indian religious culture, *bhikkhu* referred to a member of one or another monastic religious group, or to someone who became a *bhikkhu* by himself, not requiring ordination from another person or from an organized group. Many obtained *bhikkhuvesa*, the appearance of *bhikkhu*, whenever they claimed to be truthseekers.

In the Buddhist canon, particularly in the *Vinaya Piṭaka*, *bhikkhu* and *bhikkhusaṅga* refer to the religious institution of monks. The *Vinaya Piṭaka* gives two hundred twenty-seven main rules and many procedures for admission to and continuance in the *bhikkhusaṅgha*. Here, *bhikkhusaṅgha* does not denote *sāvakasaṅgha*, but the order of monks, a religious institution rather than a community of spiritually advanced disciples.

Although *bhikkhusaṅgha* is not essentially *sāvakasaṅgha,* its members are already *sāvakas,* as *sāvakas* ordinarily means disciples or followers. In the Theravāda tradition there are four groups of *sāvakas: bhikkhus, bhikkhunīs, upāsakas,* and *upāsikās. Bhikkhus* are ordained male disciples; *bhikkhunīs* are ordained female disciples; *upāsakas* and *upāsikās* are male and female lay disciples respectively. All of them follow the eightfold path. In any of these four groups of followers, one or more persons may already have reached a spiritually sublime state, even one of the eight stages, and any such would already belong to the *sāvakasaṅgha* of the triple gem. Let us carefully note, then, that some members of the institutional order of monks may belong to the triple gem *sāvakasaṅgha,* but if so, their spiritual attainment rather than their ordination qualified them. All members of the order of monks hold their membership in the institutional order simply by virtue of their qualifications for ordination. However, in the community of the eight noble states, *i.e.,* in the *sāvakasaṅgha* of the triple gem, those unordained ones as well as ordained, both male and female, belong by virtue of advanced purity of mind.

Although the canonical texts abound in references to lay male and female *sāvakas* (disciples), we have not as yet found in these texts any expression such as *upāsakasaṅgha* (male lay disciple community) or *upāsikāsaṅgha* (female lay disciple community) which would correspond to *bhikkhusaṅgha* and *bhikkhunīsaṅgha,* respectively the community of ordained male and ordained female disciples. We draw no inferences about this apparent absence of a specific term for an institutional community of lay disciples. We merely register here our intellectual curiosity about this seeming absence.

In Theravāda Buddhist countries the yellow robe identifies the ordained person more certainly than the white frocks identify the lay persons who on appointed occasions observe the eight precepts. But clothing makes neither a saintly monk nor a saintly lay person, although the yellow robe attests to the vows taken by the ascetic who observes *Vinaya* rules and the special all-white garments attest the precept observance of lay persons. A passage in the *Majjhima-nikāya* counsels against confusing robes with righteousness:

> I say it is not the robe nor nakedness which makes the ascetic. . . . If merely wearing the robe could banish greed, malice, and so forth, then as soon as a baby is born his family and friends should make him wear the robe and insist that he wear it, saying, 'Come now, thou favored of fortune! Come put on the robe, for by the mere wearing of the robe the greedy get rid of their greed, the malicious get rid of their malice.'[10]

Neither ordination nor robes, nor householding nor white frocks have any inherent spiritual power for the follower of the path. We have shown sufficient textual evidence to refute any suggestions that the Theravāda tradition presents a system of self-discipline designed exclusively or even primarily for the yellow-robed monks. We find in the Theravāda texts a plan for mental purification, not a movement for monastic ascetics. Although some Theravādins pursue that plan while living the ascetic life, the objective of the Theravāda is not the multiplication of monks.

We do not deny that in Theravāda cultures the yellow-robed monk has received from the masses an uncritical respect. In the mentality of the masses the monk has represented a holier existence than that thought possible for laymen. This respect has not lacked foundation in the people's experience, however. Monks at the village temple or at temples in the towns and cities have befriended the people, counseled and comforted them in the adversities common to humans, and monks have helped them to create circumstances warranting joyful community celebration. The Venerable Professor Walpola Sri Rahula has described the magnanimous actions of monks who worked on behalf of the people's health, education, and general welfare. One will have to search long to find a leadership figure which excels that of the monks described in Rahula's *The Heritage of the Bhikkhu*.[11] But having acknowledged with commensurate praise the compassionate labors and the spiritual guidance and influence of the monks, we are left with the conclusion that doctrinally speaking, monasticism does not constitute the religious objective of the Theravāda tradition.

Realization of nibbāna constitutes the highest and ultimate goal of Buddhist doctrine and aspiration. Therefore laymen and monks alike should aspire to becoming one of the noble persons, destined for perfect enlightenment. Lay life offers no impediment to fulfilling this noble aspiration. King Bimbisāra became a stream-winner, but he did not take monastic ordination either beforehand or afterwards. Indeed, he made a declaration to remain a lay disciple even after his realization: "Lord, may the Blessed One accept me as a lay-disciple gone for refuge from this day forth for as long as life lasts."[12] Here Bimbisāra, a stream entrant, reciting the triple gem, used the expression *bhikkhusaṅgha*. Such persons do not publicly claim to belong to the community of eight blessed persons.

Earlier in this chapter we saw that hundreds of lay disciples achieved one of the blessed states and, numbered among the four pairs, remained in the life of the laity. These evidences disclose to us that the difference between a layman's life-style and that of a monk does not figure substantively in the realization of nibbāna. The possibility of realization which is accessible to the monk is also accessible to the layman. The means or path of realizing nibbāna is the same for laymen as for monks.

Clearly no one has to take refuge exclusively in the ordained ones when taking refuge in the sangha of the triple gem. This Buddhist practice can be misunderstood by those who have been brought up in religious traditions practicing baptismal and confessional rites. Taking refuge, reciting the formula expressing veneration for the Buddha, the dhamma, and the sangha of beatified ones, does not parallel confessing the Apostles' Creed in Christianity. One does not have formally to take refuge in the triple gem in order to follow the eightfold path realized and taught by the Buddha. Neither can a monk or anyone else transmit sacramental powers which would qualify a person to become one of the eight noble ones.

Buddhists do practice the rite of transferring merits, compassionately giving to another whatever merit one has gained from meritorious actions. But such merit alone could never advance another to one of the blessed states. Taking refuge in the triple gem does not evoke a divine grace, or the Buddha's grace, or the Buddha's spirit, either literally or symbolically. Faith in the sangha does not even require formally taking the refuges. When a person sees the Truth s/he simultaneously gains confidence in all those who previously have understood the Truth because now s/he has perceived the Truth her/himself. S/he realizes that s/he has the realization of Truth in common with these others. The community of blessed disciples increases by individuals sparately realizing nibbāna to the extent of assuring their ultimate perfection. The only reliable authority, ultimately, in the Buddhist tradition is the authority of one's own experience of Truth.

When the Buddha sent out the enlightened ones to preach the Truth, he sent them because they were enlightened, not because they had received ordination to preach the dhamma or to perform rites initiating converts into something called Buddhism. Both lay disciples and monks hold, on a parity basis, the responsibility to propagate the dhamma. The Buddha made clear his conviction on this:

> I shall not die, O Evil One! until the brethren and sisters of the Order, and *until the lay-disciples of both male and female sex shall have become true hearers,* wise and well trained, ready and learned, carrying the doctrine in their memory, masters of the lesser corollaries that follow from the larger doctrine, correct in life, having lived according to the precepts — *until they, having thus themselves learned the doctrine, shall be able to tell others of it, preach it, make it known,* establish it, open it, minutely explain it, and make it clear.[13]

Buddhist ordination admits individuals into the order of monks, and ordination merely means to accept acceptance into the order by its members. In the beginning of the order, the Buddha addressed certain truth-seekers and said to them, "Come, monks," and that constituted the entirety of their ordination. "'Come, monks,' the Lord said, 'well taught is the dhamma, fare the Brahmafaring for making an utter end of ill.' So this was these venerable ones' ordination."[14] Ordination originally was just that simple, but it developed into more formal rituals. It came to involve a nomination process in which a candidate's name was moved three times in the presence of a prescribed number of monks:

> From this day forth, monks, I abolish that ordination gained by going to the refuges and which I allowed. I allow you, monks, to ordain by a (formal) act consisting of a motion and a resolution put three times.[15]

These references illustrate that Buddhist ordination has, from the beginning and in its further development, consisted in the acceptance of a person, originally by the Buddha himself and subsequently by the order of monks, into the order of monks.

Why should anyone become a Buddhist monk? What, if any, advantage does the monastic life have over the lay life? The answer to each of these questions is practical rather than doctrinal.

Fundamentally, ordination distinguishes the monk from the householder by the kind of life which the monk agrees to live in response to his acceptance by and into the monastic order. The monk both requests and agrees to live his life henceforth following the rules of the *Vinaya Piṭaka* as he pursues the path to nibbāna. Gotama Buddha and some of his disciples preferred the practical alternative of living the monastic life, the rules for which later generations recorded in the *Vinaya Piṭaka*. In choosing to become monks they expressed a personal preference shared by many Buddhists to this day. The Buddha stated his own preference simply: "I became a monk seeing lay life as a barrier but monkhood as open air."[16] Some of the Buddha's disciples who became monks considered the household life a path for the dust of passion:

> Free as the air is the life of him who has renounced all worldly things. Let me then cut off my hair and beard, let me clothe myself in the orange-coloured robes, and let me go forth from the household life into the homeless state.[17]

While we may discern an implicit value judgment in the Buddha's statement and that made by some of his disciples, the value judgments are private and personal, not institutionally legislated.

A person assumes the ascetic life prescribed in the *Vinaya* rules and counsels in order to spend more time in meditation and service to others than he would have in the householder's routine. One steps forth from the householder's life not primarily to seek ordination, but to gain the advantage of time and the kind of religious environment he considers most advantageous for living his life virtuously, for pursuing religious study, and for practicing meditation. Ordination signifies the ordinand's avowed preference and recognized readiness for the ascetic way of advancing his own understanding and practice of the dhamma.

Becoming a monk improves one's opportunity for advancing in knowledge and practice of the dhamma only if the individual perceives it so. Others may prefer the householder's responsibilities over the *Vinaya* regimen not because they lack the fortitude to adhere to the exacting *Vinaya* demands, but because with religious sincerity they perceive the householder's life as holding for them the best opportunity to advance in knowledge and practice of the dhamma. In the case of the layman, as in the case of the monk, the individual makes the decision independently if he makes it religiously in the Buddhist sense rather than becoming a householder merely by failure to consider religiously the alternatives of monastic and lay life.

We can now repeat, and answer briefly but adequately, our two questions. Why should anyone become a Buddhist monk? What, if any, advantage does the monastic life have over the lay life? Anyone who finds the monastic routine prescribed by the *Vinaya* best suited to his own disposition and inclinations should become a monk. For such persons the monastic practices will enable them to advance more rapidly in the wisdom and compassion of the dhamma. For others, the householder's life will offer no impediment to spiritual growth. So, we conclude, the individual's spiritual discernment will determine for him whether the monastic or the householder's mode of life offers the greater advantage. For some persons membership in the *bhikkusaṅgha* offers a practical alternative but not a doctrinal necessity for advancement on the path to perfection. For others, the householder's life affords ample opportunity for the same kind of spiritual advancement, again as a personal and practical alternative and not as a doctrinal necessity.

For householder and monastic, the *sāvakasaṅgha* of the triple gem constitutes a doctrinal necessity, namely, the necessity of realizing nibbāna as one of the blessed persons. The path leading to that sangha of blessed persons is a path of mental purification which may be pursued as successfully through family life responsibilities as through monastic regimen. The respect rendered monks in Buddhist cultures and the conventional identification of the *bhikkhusaṅgha* with the *sāvakasaṅgha* (even by so enlightened a person as King Bimbisāra) has no bearing upon the distinction of the spiritual path from either the monk's ascetic practices or the householder's round of duties. Monasticism counts for nothing; householding counts for nothing. Purifying the mind counts for everything. Consequently we close our essay with one Vacchagotta's inquiry and the Buddha's response:

> Let be the good Gotama. Has the good Gotama even one monk who is a disciple and who, by the destruction of the cankers, having realized here and now by his own super-knowledge the freedom of mind and the freedom through intuitive wisdom that are cankerless, entering on them is abiding in them?
>
> Not merely a hundred, Vaccha, nor two hundred, three hundred, four hundred, nor five hundred, but far more are those monks, disciples of mine, who, by the destruction of the cankers, having realized here and now by their own super-knowledge the freedom of mind and the freedom through intuitive wisdom that are cankerless, entering on them are abiding in them.
>
> Let be the good Gotama, let be the monks. But has the good Gotama even one nun who is a disciple and who, by the destruction of the cankers, having realized here and now by her own super-knowledge the freedom of mind and the freedom through intuitive wisdom that are cankerless, entering on them is abiding in them?
>
> Not merely a hundred, Vacca, nor two, three, four, or five hundred, but far more are those nuns, disciples of mine, who, by the destruction of the cankers, having here and now realized by their own super-knowledge the freedom of mind and the freedom through intuitive wisdom that are cankerless, entering on them are abiding in them.
>
> Let be the good Gotama, let be the monks, let be the nuns. But has the good Gotama even one layfollower who is a disciple, a householder clothed in white, a Brahma-farer who, by the utter destruction of the five fetters binding to this lower (shore) is of spontaneous uprising, one who has attained nibbāna there and is not liable to return from that world?
>
> Not merely a hundred, Vaccha, not . . . five hundred, but far more are those layfollowers, disciples of mine, householders clothed in white, Brahma-farers, who by the utter destruction of the five fetters binding to this lower (shore), are of spontaneous uprising, those who have attained nibbāna there and are not liable to return from that world!'[18]

A Metaphor

The Buddha is like one who passes down the inheritance of Dhamma: Dhamma True is like that inheritance; the Sangha, which is like a group of children who are heirs of an inheritance, is heir to the inheritance of Dhamma True.

dhammadāyajjasampadānako viya buddho,
dāyajjam viya saddhammo, dāyajjadāyādo
puttavaggo viya saddhammadāyajjadāyādo saṃgho.

Paramatthajotikā I
(the commentary on the *Khuddaka-Pāṭha*). p. 22

Notes and References

Notes to Chapter 1

1. This chapter was presented in a slightly abridged form at the 30th International Congress for Human Science in Asia and North Africa in Mexico City on Thursday, August 5, 1976. It was published as Chapter 5 in A. K. Narain, ed., *Studies in Pali and Buddhism* (Delhi: B. R. Publishing Corporation, 1979), pp. 41-52, and appears here in a slightly revised form, and with the kind permission of A. K. Narain and the B. R. Publishing Corporation.

2. The authors of the chapters in this volume differ in choice of English style and word usage. Most noticeable is the absence or presence of the English definite article before Dhamma and the use of capitals in Dhamma/dhamma and Sangha /sangha.

Taking the latter case first, the issue of whether or not to utilize English capital letters in Dhamma (as in Chapters I, II, and III)/dhamma (as in Chapter IV) and Sangha (as in Chapters I, II, and III)/sangha (as in Chapter IV) represents primarily preference in style. The lower case usage should not be construed as reflecting a conceptual fragmentation of the integral relationship of these two dimensions of the threefold refuge.

The case of whether to use the definite article before Dhamma is more subtle; the reader will note its absence in Chapters I and III. I am aware that its absence will tend to strike the English reader, at first blush, as being somewhat unusual; possibly because of the presence of the definite article with the other nouns in the threefold refuge and also because of its near standard presence in almost all books in English of and about Buddhists.

I have not used the definite article before Dhamma for a number of reasons, a full elaboration of which would require a lengthy statement. The main point at issue is that, within the English context, the definite article tends a little too directly toward specificity when used as the sole adjectival modifier of the term Dhamma and this tendency might be misleading in two significant ways.

The use of the definite article, as in "the Dhamma," might suggest a thing or something particularized. (1) It, "the Dhamma," might suggest a particular doctrine among others, a particular idea among others. As the term occurs in the threefold refuge, it does designate a particular idea, of course. But part of the subtle and important force of this particular idea is discerned in nuance, in delicate connotations that are evoked when a Buddhist becomes engaged with it. The definite article might restrict this dimension or might lead a reader not to be aware of it. (2) It, "the Dhamma," might suggest to an English-speaking reader something particularized in another sense; that "the Dhamma" is something which Buddhists have or which Buddhists do. However, Buddhists tend to avoid implications of possessiveness while averring that following

Dhamma is eminently worthwhile. They have discerned through the term, through the idea, concept, that which is universal, is available to all persons, is not readily particularized.

The point might be seen rather quickly by drawing to our attention what others, who have written in English, have already sensed about the testimony of Buddhists: rarely will one see the definite article before *dukkha* or *paññā*, rarer still before Nibbāna, when these terms stand alone without other accompanying, particularizing phrases. Apparently, these writers have discerned the Buddhist witness that these notions are relevant to all persons. The point is the same in the case of Dhamma.

I have continued the use of the definite article before "Buddha," and "Sangha" because they both are particular proper nouns.

3. *V.* I.4, referring to two male lay devotees, *upāsakas.*

4. *JāA.*, I.80-81.

5. *Upāsakajanālaṅkara*, ed. by H. Saddhatissa (London: Published for the Pali Text Society, Luzac & Co., Ltd., 1965), Chapter I, p. 44.

6. *Śri Saddharmāvavāda Saṃgrahaya*, ed. by Vēragoḍa Amaramoli Thera (Colombo: Ratnākara Mudraṇālayaya, 1956), p. 77.

7. *Jātaka Aṭuvā Gäṭapadaya*, ed. by Mäda-Uyangoḍa Vimalakīrti Thera and Nähinnē Sominda Thera (Colombo: M. D. Gunasena & Co., 1961), p. 47 (on *JāA.*, I.81.1).

8. *V.* I.16-17, referring to an *upāsaka*, and, *ibid.*, p. 18, referring to an *upāsikā*, a female lay devotee.

9. See, for example *SnA.*, I.216 (on *Sn.* vs. 180); *SA*, I.81 (on *S.* I.215).

10. See the discussion by Edmund F. Perry and Shanta Ratnayaka in Chapter IV, "The Sangha as Refuge."

11. *KhpA.*, p. 170 (on the Ratanasutta [see also *Sn.*, vs. 224]).

12. *MA.* I.131-132. See also *AA.* II.108-112; *DA.*, I.229-234; and *KhpA.*, pp. 16-17. I have chosen to follow the *MA.* (which is the same as the *AA.* and *DA.* accounts) because it is more concise than the *KhpA.* See the complementary discussion by George D. Bond drawn primarily from *KhpA.* in Chapter II, and especially his comparative analysis of the two modes of presentation reflected in these sources. The commentarial explanation in *MA.* has been rather freely translated into English by Nyāṇaponika Thera as *The Threefold Refuge in* "The Wheel Series," No. 76 (Kandy, Ceylon [Sri Lanka]: Buddhist Publication Society, 1965 [first published by the "Servants of the Buddha," 1949). *KhpA.* has been reliably translated into English by Bhikkhu Ñāṇamoli in the Pali Text Society translation series, No. 32, as *The Minor Readings and the Illustrator of Ultimate Meaning* (London: Luzac & Co., Ltd., 1960).

13. *MA.* I.132. So, too, *KhpA.*, p. 16. See also *Vaṃsatthappakāsinī: Commentary on the Mahāvaṃsa*, ed. by G. P. Malalasekera for the Government of Ceylon (London: Published for the Pali Text Society by Humphrey Milford, Oxford University Press, 1935); Vol. I. 308 (on *Mahāvaṃsa*, Chapter XI, vs. 35), and *Dharmapradīpikā*, ed. by Baddēgama Vimalavaṃsa Thera, 2nd ed. (Colombo: M. D. Guṇasēna & Co., 1967), pp. 179-183, a Sinhala version of the

MA. passage, and *BuA*., pp. 122-123. This last source makes it clear that the commentators tended, for homiletical purposes, to take *saraṇa* as being derived from the root *śr*, "to crush," as in the following: "*sarati hiṃsati vināsetī ti saranam*," "it crushes, slays, destroys, hence [the meaning of] *saraṇa*." The term *saraṇa* can be derived, of course, from the root *śri*, "to resort." See also Bond's comments in Chapter II, p. 23.

14. As previously stated in my *Dhamma: Western Academic and Sinhalese Buddhist Interpretations – a study of a religious concept* (Tokyo: The Hokuseido Press, 1978), note 73, p. 84.

15. C. A. F. Rhys Davids, *A Manual of Buddhism: For Advanced Students* (London: The Sheldon Press, 1932), p. 60.

16. Wilfred Cantwell Smith, "Religious Atheism? Early Buddhist and Recent American," *Milla wa-Milla*, No. 6 (December, 1966), p. 9. The Buddhist segment of this article has been published, with some revision, as Chapter 2: "The Buddhist Instance: Faith as Atheist?" in Wilfred Cantwell Smith, *Faith and Belief* (Princeton: Princeton University Press, 1979); see p. 25 for the phrase quoted in the text.

17. See *MA*. II.113 (on *M*. I.138); *Sdpj*. I.74 (on *Mahāniddesa* 1.I.17); and *SnA*. I.151 (on *Sn*. vs. 80).

18. *MA*. I.132 (on *M*. I.24).

19. *Ibid*., p. 131.

20. See the discussion of the force of *śraddhā* (*saddhā*) by Wilfred Cantwell Smith in his Chapter 4 of *Faith and Belief*, pp. 59-68.

21. See, for example, the commentarial discussion at *KhpA*., p. 183 (on *Sn*., vs. 227); *DA*. I.181 (on *D*. I.5), *ThagA*., II.71 (on *Thag*., vs. 204), II.102 (on *Thag*., vs. 249), and III.41 (on *Thag*., vs. 789).

22. *MA*., I.132.

23. *Ibid*.

24. *Ibid*., p. 133.

25. *Ibid*.

26. *S*. II.220.

27. *MA*. I.133, quoting from *Sn*., vs. 192.

28. *MA*. I.133, quoting from *M*. II.144.

29. See the discussion of this matter by Bond in Chapter II, pp. 25.

30. *MA*. I.133.

31. *Ibid*., p. 134.

32. *Ibid*.

33. One might seize upon a standard polarity of "ordinary" and "extraordinary," as has been done occasionally since the appearance of Franklin Edgerton's article, "Dominant Ideas in the Formation of Indian Culture," *Journal of the American Oriental Society*, Vol. 62 (Sept. 1942), p. 155. The word *ordinary* has, for our purposes, an unfortunate connotation of "inferior." *Customary* tends to avoid this connotational drift and carries an additional relevance of suggesting an activity of a community.

34. *MA.* I.134. See the brief presentation of the categories of the eight noble persons, who have attained the four paths and four fruits, given by Perry and Ratnayaka in Chapter IV, pp. 43-44.

35. *MA.* I.132. Note that in this *lokuttarasaraṇagamana* one "roots out what harms this going for refuge," (*saraṇagamanūpakkilesamuccheda*), whereas in the *lokiya* going for refuge, one only arrests (*vikkhambhana*) what harms the process.

36. *Ibid.*

37. *Ibid.*, I.134. The quotation is from the *Dhammapada* (PTS edition), vss. 190-192.

38. Compare a related passage in the *Dhammapada*, vss. 277-279.

39. *MA.* I.134. The quotation is from *A.* I.26-27.

40. *MA.* I.135. *DhpA.* III.246 (on *Dhp.* vss. 190-192) focuses on the worship of the teachers, *etc.*, as an example of how refuge, either that taken by a householder or by one who has "gone forth" into monastic life, can be shaken; not so, however, for one who has a vision of the immovable state (*acalabhāvan*), *i.e.*, Nibbāna (Dhamma / Nibbāna).

Notes to Chapter II

1. A preliminary version of this chapter was first presented to a breakfast group at the annual meeting of the American Academy of Religion, 1979.

2. Max Weber, *The Religion of India: The Sociology of Hinduism and Buddhism*, trans. and ed. by H. Gerth and D. Martindale (New York: The Free Press, 1958), p. 206.

3. This point is demonstrated by John Ross Carter in "The Notion of Refuge (*Saraṇa*) in the Theravāda Buddhist Tradition," above Chapter I.

4. For example, the word "refuge," *saraṇa*, is the same word used in the *Bhagavadgītā*, (18.66) to refer to Krishna, who declares, "turn to me as your only refuge and I will deliver you from all evils." The Theravāda tradition has not, however, meant what the *Bhagavadgītā* meant by refuge, but it clearly has regarded going for refuge in the Buddha as part of the path leading to release from all suffering.

5. *D.* II.82-83.

6. *S.* III.120.

7. *D.* II.138.

8. *V.* I.4; *D.* II.152.

9. *V.* I.22.

10. *KhpA.*, p. 14.

11. *D.* I.110, 124-125, 147; *M.* I.24.

12. *M.* II.90, 162.

13. *D.* I.99; cf. *MA.* I.133.

14. *KhpA.*, p. 14.

15. *Vism.*, p. 198.

16. *KhpA.*, p. 14; *MA.* I.171.

17. *The Majjhima-Nikāya,* Vol. I, 386.

18. *Vism.*, pp. 201-202.

19. Buddhaghosa's explanation of this term, *lokavidū,* includes an interesting catalogue of the cosmological and geographical wisdom of ancient India. See *Vism.*, pp. 204-207.

20. I. B. Horner, trans., *The Collection of the Middle Length Sayings (Majjhima-Nikāya),* Vol. II (London: Published for the Pali Text Society by Luzac & Company, Ltd., 1957), n. 9, p. 51.

21. *KhpA.*, p. 15.

22. See *ibid.*, and *Vism.*, p. 202.

23. T. W. Rhys Davids termed this kind of commentarial etymology "fanciful etymology." But this etymology has a valid purpose in the commentaries for it aims to establish the doctrinal rather than the philological meaning. See also the observation by Carter above in note 13 to Chapter I and in the discussion on Dhamma, in Chapter III, pp. 35-36.

24. *Vism.*, p. 201.

25. *KhpA.*, pp. 14-15.

26. *M.* I.171; *V.* I.8.

27. *M.* I.171.

28. *Vism.*, p. 207.

29. *A.* II.37-39.

30. *M.* I.386.

31. *KhpA.*, p. 15; *Vism.*, p. 210.

32. *M.* I.386.

33. *S.* I.67.

34. Venerable Nyāṇaponika Thera, "Devotion in Buddhism I," *Devotion in Buddhism,* Wheel Publication, No. 18 (Kandy: The Buddhist Publication Society, 1975), p. 8.

35. *S.* I.139.

36. *S.* II.103-104.

37. *S.* I.138 ff. See also Carter, *Dhamma: Western Academic . . .,* pp. 78-83.

38. *Vism.*, p. 203.

39. *M.* I.21, 83.

40. *Vism.*, p. 208.

41. Winston King, *Buddhism and Christianity: Some Bridges of Understanding* (London: Allen and Unwin, 1963), p.52.

42. *S.* V.442.

43. *KhpA.*, p. 14.

44. *MA.* I.130-131; *KhpA.*, p. 18-19.

45. *MA.* I.132; *KhpA.*, p. 16.

46. See the observation by Carter in note 13 to Chapter I, above.

47. *KhpA.*, pp. 18-19.

48. *Ibid.*, p. 18.

49. *Ibid.*, pp. 18-19; cf. *MA.* I.130-131.

50. *KhpA.*, p. 19; *MA.* I.131. See the translation by Carter on p. 6 of Chapter I, above.

51. See above Chapter I, p. 2.

52. *DA*. I.229-234; *MA*. I.132-133; *AA*. II.109-110.

53. *KhpA*., pp. 16-17.

54. For purposes of giving references to this version of the commentarial explanation of the *tisaraṇa*, we shall cite the page numbers in the *MA*. only.

55. Venerable Nyāṇaponika, *The Threefold Refuge*, Wheel Publication No. 76 (Kandy: Buddhist Publication Society, 1965), p. 17.

56. *MA*. I.132 and parallels.

57. KhpA., p. 17; *MA*. I.133.See also the observation by Carter, Chapter I, pp. 9.

58. *KhpA*., p. 16; *MA*. I.133.

59. Nyāṇaponika, *op. cit*., note, p. 5.

60. *KhpA*., pp. 16-17; *MA*. I.133; *M*. II.133-146. See the translation by Carter, of the related passage from *MA*., above Chapter I, p. 000.

61. Nyāṇaponika, *op. cit*., p. 17.

62. *MA*. I.132.

63. Donald K. Swearer, "The Appeal of Buddhism: A Christian Perspective," *The Christian Century* LXXXVIII, No. 44 (Nov. 3, 1971), p. 129.

64. *Ibid*., p. 129.

65. Winston L. King, *In the Hope of Nibbāna* (Lasalle, Illinois: Open Court Publishing Co., 1964), p. 13.

66. *KhpA*., p. 17.

67. *MA*. I.132. See on this the discussion by Carter above, in Chapter I, pp. 12-13.

68. *MA*. I.132-133.

69. Interestingly, the two commentarial accounts appear to diverge somewhat about the nature of the fruits of mundane refuge. Both *KphA*. and *MA*. (and parallels) cite a passage from *D*. II.255 which says "those who go for refuge to the Buddha will not go to states of woe after death" (*KhpA*., p. 17; *MA*. I.134). *MA*. and its parallels take this passage as a guarantee of the fruits of mundane refuge. But KhpA. says that the passage refers to beings on the supramundane path only. This is another example of an apparent independence of these two streams of the commentarial tradition.

70. *MA*. I.134-135.

71. *Dhp*., vs. 276.

72. See *M*. III.4-5.

73. See *M*. II.169-170.

74. *D*. II.100.

75. *Dhp*., vss. 188-192.

76. M. I.169.

77. Wilfred Cantwell Smith, "Religious Atheism? Early Buddhist and Recent American," *Milla wa-Milla*, 6 (Dec. 1966), p. 13. The Buddhist segment of this article has been published, with some revision, as Chapter 2: "The Buddhist Instance: Faith as Atheist?" in Wilfred Cantwell Smith, *Faith and Belief*

(Princeton: Princeton University Press, 1979); see pp. 29-30 for the phrase quoted in our text.

78. *Ibid.*, (*Milla wa-Milla*, p. 12; *Faith and Belief*, p. 28).

79. John Ross Carter, "Dhamma as a Religious Concept: A Brief Investigation of Its History in the Western Academic Tradition and Its Centrality Within the Sinhalese Theravāda Tradition," *Journal of the American Academy of Religion*, 44, 4 (1976), p. 670. See, further, Chapter III.

80. *Ud.*, p. 80.

81. For further discussion of this idea, see Robert L. Slater, *Paradox and Nirvana: a study of religious ultimates with special reference to Burmese Buddhism* (Chicago: The University of Chicago Press, 1951). Carter, in *Dhamma: Western Academic and Sinhalese Buddhist Interpretations — a study of a religious concept* (Tokyo: The Hokuseido Press, 1978), pp. 176-177, says of Slater's work that, "In the course of his study he spoke of a relationship between *dhamma* and *nibbāna* and noted that whether or not *nibbāna* was taken as 'the consummating, central term of Buddhism' depends on the suggestive significance one assigns to *dhamma* [R. L. Slater, *Paradox and Nirvāna*, n. 76, p. 63]." Carter concludes, "Slater was near the mark when he said *nibbāna* was the 'consummating' term. My point is that Sinhalese Buddhists have said that the relationship between the concept *dhamma* and the notion *nibbāna* is integral."

82. Smith, "Religious Atheism?" *Milla wa-Milla*, p. 12 (*Faith and Belief*, p. 28).

83. Bhikkhu V. Buddharakkhita, "Devotion in Buddhism II," *Devotion in Buddhism*, Wheel Publication No. 18 (Kandy: Buddhist Publication Society, 1960), p. 15.

Notes to Chapter III

1. This chapter was originally presented as a paper entitled "*Dhamma* in the *Tisarana*," at the annual Midwest meeting of the American Academy of Religion, held at Northwestern University, on February 16, 1979. It appears here with minor revisions.

2. *Pānadurē Vādaya*, ed. by P. A. Peiris and James Dias (Colombo: Lanka Free Press, n.d.), p. 43. See also *Buddhism and Christianity: Being an Oral Debate at Panadura between the Rev. Migettiwatte Gunananda & the Rev. David de Silva*; Introduction and annotation by J. M. Peebles (Colombo: Mahabodhi Press, n.d.). I have discussed this general topic of Dhamma as refuge at some length in *Dhamma: Western Academic and Sinhalese Buddhist Interpretations — a study of a religious concept* (Tokyo: The Hokuseido Press, 1978), pp. 159 ff, and n. 9, p. 159 for the Sinhala.

3. See E. Burnouf, *Introduction à l'histoire du bouddhisme indien* (Paris: Imprimerie Royale, 1844), n. 2, p. 80. Henri Arvon, *Buddhism*, translated by Douglas Scott (New York: Walker & Co., 1964]of the work first published as *Le Bouddhisme*, 1951]), p. 51.

4. Robert Lawson Slater, *Paradox and Nirvana: a study of religious ultimates with special reference to Burmese Buddhism* (Chicago: The University of Chicago Press, 1951), p. 132. Piyadassi Thera, *The Buddha's Ancient Path* (London: Rider & Company, 1964), p. 20. Walpola Sri Rahula, *What the Buddha Taught* (revised edition, Bedford, England: Gordon Fraser, 1967), p. 8. Dhamma, in this context, is taken as "die Lehr" by Magdalene and Wilhelm Geiger, *Pāli Dhamma: vornehmlich in der kanonischen Literatur* (München: Verlag der Bayerischen Akademie der Wissenschaften, 1920), p. 58.

5. *The Pali Text Society's Pali-English Dictionary*, ed. by T. W. Rhys Davids and William Stede (London: Luzac & Co., Ltd., 1966), p. 337b. These editors also noted Dhamma in this context as meaning "the 'Word,' the Wisdom or Truth." Noting the meaning of Dhamma here as "Doctrine" are also Richard Gombrich, *Precept and Practice: Traditional Buddhism in the Rural Highlands of Ceylon* (Oxford: Clarendon Press, 1971), p. 64; so also Kitsiri Malalgoda, *Buddhism in Sinhalese Society 1750-1900: a Study of Religious Revival and Change* (Berkeley: University of California Press, 1976), p. 26; Christmas Humphreys, *Buddhism* (Hammondsworth, Middlesex: Penguin Books, Ltd., 1958), p. 242. See also H. Saddhatissa, *Buddhist Ethics: Essence of Buddhism* (London: George Allen & Unwin Ltd., 1970), p. 58.

6. B. Clough, *A Sinhalese-English Dictionary* (New and enlarged edition, Colombo: Wesleyan Mission Press, 1892), p. 269a (*s. v. dharmaratnaya*); R. Spence Hardy, *Eastern Monachism* (London: Partridge and Oakey, 1850), pp. 166-167; Mrs. C. A. F. Rhys Davids, *Buddhism: A Study of the Buddhist Norm* (London: William and Norgate, n.d., [1912]), p. 235; A. B. Keith, *Buddhist Philosophy in India and Ceylon* (Oxford: Clarendon Press, 1923), p. 133.

7. See the immediately preceding four notes (3-6). These sources and authors are here listed as being merely representative of a tendency, perhaps, not to communicate to readers the depth of meaning Dhamma represents in this context. And, certainly, there are other writers who have provided such interpretations as noted above. Certainly, too, it cannot be said of all the writers noted that they represent merely so-called popularizers or amateurs.

8. *Pānadurē Vādaya, op. cit.*, p. 76. See also Carter, *Dhamma*, pp. 159-160, and n. 11, p. 160 for the Sinhala.

9. For Pāli commentarial references, see, for example, *MA*. I.130-131; *AA*. II.107-108; *Upāsakajanālaṅkāra* ed. by H. Saddhatissa (London: Published for the Pali Text Society by Luzac & Co., Ltd., 1965), Chapter I, paragraphs 67-68. For occurrence in Sinhala sources, see *Saddharmaratnāvaliya* (13th century), ed. by Kiriällē Ñāṇavimala Thera (Colombo: M. D. Guṇasēna, 1961), pp. 34, 520; *Saddharmālaṅkara* (14th century), ed. by Kiriällē Ñāṇavimala Thera (Colombo: M. D. Guṇasēna, 1954), pp. 19, 93, 106, 229, 418, 780; *Saddharmaratnākaraya* (ca. 15th century), ed. by Kalupaluvāvē Devānanda Thera (Colombo: Ratnākara Pot Veḷanda Śālāva, 1955), pp. 61, 212, 266, 298, 531; *Saddharma Sārārtha Saṃgrahaya* (1726), ed. by Kiriällē Ñāṇavimala Thera (Colombo: M. D. Guṇasēna, 1957), pp. 352, 353, 442; *Śrī Saddharmāvavāda Saṃgrahaya* (1773), ed. by Vēragoḍa Amaramoli Thera (Colombo: Ratnākara Mudraṇālayaya, 1956), pp. 2, 468.

10. Māpalagama Siri Somissara, *Bauddha Dharma Mārgaya* (Colombo: Vijayasēna saha Sahōdaraya, 1967), pp. 185-186; Rērukānē Candavimala, *Pohoya Dinaya* (Colombo: A. D. P. Sugatadasa, Anula Mudraṇālaya, 1966), pp. 30-32; Rērukānē Chandavimala, *Sūvisi Maha Guṇaya* (Colombo: A. D. P. Sugatadasa, Anula Mudraṇālaya, 1969), pp. 429 *passim*. And there are others.

11. On the "twofold" and "threefold" formulas, see above, Chapter I, and notes 3-8 to Chapter I for sources. On the important term *sāvakasaṅgha*, see the discussion by Edmund F. Perry and Shanta Ratnayaka, Chapter IV.

12. *MA*. I.131; *AA*. II.107.

13. Compare the interpretation of *saraṇa* mentioned in note 13 to Chapter I, and George D. Bond's observation in note 23 to Chapter II.

14. *MA*. I.173; "*Dhāraṇato dhammo. Vinipatitum appadānato ti vuttaṃ hoti.*"

15. *Dhammapāla's Paramattha-Dīpanī*, Part IV, Being the Commentary on the *Vimāna-Vatthu*, ed. by E. Hardy (London: Published for the Pali Text Society by Henry Frowde, Oxford University Press, 1901), p. 232.

16. *KhpA.*, p. 19.

17. *Upāsakajanālaṅkāra* (PTS edition), Chapter I, paragraph 66.

18. *Paramattha-Dīpanī Udānaṭṭhakathā (Udāna Commentary) of Dhammapālācariya*, ed. by F. L.Woodward (London: Published for the Pali Text Society by the Oxford University Press, 1926), p. 268.

19. *Śrī Saddharmavavāda Saṃgrahaya, op. cit.*, p. 273.

20. On the meaning of *sāvakasaṅgha*, see the more sustained study by Perry and Ratnayaka in Chapter IV.

21. *MA*. I.131; *AA*. II.108.

22. *Ibid.*

23. *The Vimāna-Vatthu: of the Khuddaka Nikāya Sutta Piṭaka*, ed. by Edmund Rowland Gooneratne (London: Published for the Pali Text Society by Henry Froude [*sic.*], Oxford University Press, n.d. [1886?], p. 51. This verse is quoted at *MA*. I.131 and *AA*. II.108. See also *Upāsakajanālaṅkara* (PTS edition), Chapter I, paragraphs 67-68.

24. *MA*. I.131.

25. *Dhammapāla's Paramattha-Dīpanī*, Part IV, Being the Commentary on the *Vimāna-Vatthu* (PTS edition), p. 232.

26. *Ibid.* The Pāli reads, "*Dhamman ti sabhāvadhammaṃ. Sabhāvabhāvato gahetabbadhammo h'esa yad idaṃ maggaphalanibbānāni, na pariyattidhammo viya paññattivasena.*" I am not entirely certain about the subtleties involved in this particular distinction between *sabhāva* and *paññatti*. See *The Visuddhi-magga of Buddhaghosa*, Vol. I, ed. by C. A. F. Rhys Davids (London: Published for the Pali Text Society by Humphrey Milford, Oxford University Press, 1920), pp. 238-239, for *sabhāvadhammattā* and *sabhāvadhamme*, and *Paramatthamañjūsā of Bhadantācariya Dhammapāla Thera*: Or *The Commentary of the Vissudhimagga*, edited by Morontuduwe Dhammānanda Thera (Columbo: Mahābodhi Press, Vol. I (1928), 243, for a brief gloss

which has been translated in *The Path of Purification*, translated by Ñyānamoli (Colombo: M. D. Gunasena, 2nd edition, 1964), note 12, p. 258.

My present understanding of this distinction suggests that *paññatti* is used to designate a label or conventional concept, something that upon further analysis is discerned to be devoid of its inherent own-nature. *Sabhāva* suggests the opposite. Dhammapāla's use of *paññatti* to characterize *pariyatti-dhamma* suggests (1) that *pariyatti-dhamma*, originally meaning Dhamma to be thoroughly memorized and mastered, is being viewed as a group of composite teachings and injunctions, as textual Dhamma, and (2) that the textual Dhamma does not have its inherent own-nature, that it can perish, that it can come into existence when it is present as a text or when chanted, and can pass away from existence when the text is destroyed, when it is no longer being chanted, or, conceivably, when it is forgotten. His use of *sabhāva* to characterize the paths, fruits, and Nibbāna (known also as the *navavidhalokuttara-dhamma* – the nine-fold world transcending Dhamma) suggests that this soteriological dimension has its own inherent qualitative nature and, when one becomes engaged with it, can be relied upon.

27. *DA*. I.313; II.544.
28. *Dhp.*, vs. 178.
29. As I have attempted in a more sustained study, *Dhamma*.
30. Compare *Dhamma*, especially pp. 131-135.

Notes to Chapter IV

1. This chapter represents the results of a paper presented by the authors at the annual meeting of the American Academy of Religion in 1970. It appeared in print in 1974 under the title of "The Sangha of the Tiratana" (Occasional Paper No. 1, Religion and Ethics Institute, Inc., Evanston, Illinois). It appears here with only minor revisions and brief deletions, and with the kind permission of the Religion and Ethics Institute.
2. *M*. I.378-379.
3. See the discussion of dhamma in Chapter III above.
4. *A*. I.208.
5. *Sn*. vs. 227.
6. *S*. V.357.
7. *Ibid.*, p. 359.
8. *A*. III.211.
9. *Ibid.*, p. 212.
10. *M*. I.281-282.
11. Walpola Rahula, *The Heritage of the Bhikkhu*, tr. K. P. G. Wijayasurendra (New York: Grove Press, Inc., 1974).
12. *V*. I.37.
13. Translated from *D*. II.113. See also *Dialogues of the Buddha*, Part II, tr. T. W. and C. A. F. Rhys Davids, 4th edition (London: Published for the Pali Text Society by Luzac & Company Letd., 1959), pp. 120-121.

14. *The Book of the Discipline,* Vol. IV, tr. I. B. Horner (London: Luzac and Company Ltd., 1962), p. 56.

15. Ibid., p. 72.

16. See *Sn.*, vs. 406.

17. *Dialogues of the Buddha,* Part I, tr. T. W. Rhys Davids (London: Luzac & Company Ltd., 1956), p. 78.

18. *The Collection of the Middle Length Sayings,* Vol. II, tr. I. B. Horner (London: Published for the Pali Text Society by Luzac & Company Ltd., 1957), pp. 168-169.

Appendix 1

A Guide to English Translations of Pāli Sources Consulted in This Volume

READERS WHO have not found it practicable to set aside sufficient time to gain a reading knowledge of Pāli have access to Theravāda Buddhist canonical and commentarial literature in English translations, due in large part to the work of learned and patient scholars, most notably that of the Pāli Text Society, London. Yet, such readers, especially in the early phases of their study of this tradition, before they have acquired a thorough familiarity with the sources and literature available, frequently meet with an initial difficulty of learning the broader context of passages of the Pāli sources noted in published studies. In an attempt to overcome this difficulty, this Appendix has been included.

1. The major portions of the Pāli canonical literature have been translated into English and are noted below in this Appendix.

2. In the notes of this volume, when *A* appears as a final letter in an abbreviation, as in *SA.*, or *DhpA.*, it stands for "discourse on the meaning" (*aṭṭhakathā*), *i.e.*, it is a commentary. For example, *SA.* is the commentary on the *Saṃyutta-nikāya* and *DhpA.* is the commentary on the *Dhammapada*. In most cases, but not in all — and significantly so for this volume — the commentarial literature has not been translated into English. Listed below are English translations of important canonical and commentarial sources cited in this volume.

3. There are other commentarial sources not indicated by the letter *A*, and where English translations are available they are noted below.

Finding An English Translation of A Cited Pāli Passage

Step 1: Locating the corresponding volume in an English translation of the Pāli work cited.

Note the abbreviation or title of the Pāli text and consult the list below in Appendix I. For example, at note 5 in Notes to Chapter II, there is a reference to *D.* II.82-83. This abbreviation, listed in "Abbreviations" (provided elsewhere in this volume for cross-reference with the Bibliography) is also listed below, in this Appendix, as *D. The Dīgha-nikāya* (PTS edition) and corresponds to the English translation there listed with full bibliographical information.

Step 2: Locating the corresponding passage in an English translation.

In the English translation, note the abbreviation in the top-right of the left-side page. The abbreviation is followed by volume number and page reference. The broader context of the Pāli source (*D.* II.82-83) will be found in *Dialogues of the Buddha* (4th ed.), Part II, 87-89. In most cases, the English translations noted will also have bold-faced page numbers, within brackets in the printed text, that indicate more precisely a correspondence between the English text and the Pāli source.

Where references are made to versified texts, as, for example, *Sn.*, vs. 227, at note 5 in Notes to Chapter IV, one will be able to find another English translation located by verse number.

All translations occurring in the text of this volume are those of the authors unless otherwise indicated in the notes.

A. The Aṅguttara-nikāya (PTS edition)

The Book of the Gradual Sayings (Aṅguttara-nikāya) or More-Numbered Suttas. Vols. I-II and V, translated by F. L. Woodward, Vols, III-IV, translated by E. M. Hare, London: Published for the Pali Text Society by Luzac & Company Ltd., 1960 (Vol. I), 1962 (Vol. II), 1961 (Vol. III), 1955 (Vols. IV-V) (first published 1932-1936).

D. The Dīgha-nikāya (PTS edition)

Dialogues of the Buddha. Part I, translated by T. W. Rhys

Davids, Parts II-III, translated by T. W. Rhys Davids and C. A. F. Rhys Davids, "Sacred Books of the Buddhists," edited by F. Max Müller, Vols. II-IV, London: Luzac & Company, Ltd., 1956 (Part I), 1959 (Part II), 1957 (Part III) [first published in 1899 (Part I), 1910 (Part II), 1921 (Part III)].

Dhp. The Dhammapada (PTS edition)

Numerous are the English translations available of the *Dhammapada*. Forthcoming is a new translation of the verses and for the first time a translation of the commentarial explanations of the verses with notes translated from classical and more recent Sinhalese sources by John Ross Carter and M. Palihawa-dana.

JāA. The Jātaka: Together with Its Commentary (PTS edition)

The Jātaka or Stories of the Buddha's Former Births. Translated from the Pāli by various hands, under the editorship of Professor E. B. Cowell; Vol. I, translated by Robert Chalmers; Vol. II, by W. H. D. Rouse; Vol. III, by H. T. Francis and R. A. Neil; Vol. IV, by W. H. D. Rouse; Vol. V, by H. T. Francis; Vol. VI, an Index volume, London: Published for the Pali Text Society by Luzac & Company, Ltd., 1969 (first published 1895-1913).

KhpA. The Khuddaka-Pāṭha: Together with Its Commentary Paramatthajotikā I (PTS edition)

The Minor Readings (Kuddakapāṭha) and The Illustrator of Ultimate Meaning (Paramatthajotikā) Part I. Translated by Bhikkhu Ñāṇamoli, London: Published for the Pali Text Society by Luzac & Company, Ltd., 1960.

M. Majjhima-nikāya (PTS edition)

The Collection of The Middle Length Sayings (Majjhima-nikāya). Vols. I-III, translated by I. B. Horner, London: Published for the Pali Text Society by Luzac & Company, Ltd., 1954 (Vol. I), 1957 (Vol. II), 1959 (Vol. III).

MA. Papañcasūdanī Majjhimanikāyaṭṭhakathā: the commentary on the Majjhima-nikāya (PTS edition).

Ñyāṇaponika Thera, *The Threefold Refuge.* "The Wheel Series," No. 76, Kandy, Ceylon: Buddhist Publication Society, 1965, pp. 1-9 [first published by the "Servants of the Buddha," 1949].

S. The Saṃyutta-nikaya (PTS edition)

The Book of the Kindred Sayings (Saṃyutta-nikāya) or Grouped Suttas. Part I, translated by Mrs. Rhys Davids; Part II, translated by Mrs. Rhys Davids, assisted by F. L. Woodward; Parts III-V, translated by F. L. Woodward, London: Published for the Pali Text Society by Luzac & Company, Ltd., 1950 (Part I), 1952 (Part II), 1954 (Part III), 1956 (Parts IV-V) [first published 1917(?)-1930].

Sn. Sutta-Nipata (PTS edition)

Buddha's Teachings: Being the Sutta-Nipāta or Discourse Collection. Edited in the original Pāli Text with an English version facing it, by Lord Chalmers, Cambridge, Massachusetts: Harvard University Press, 1932.

Woven Cadences of Early Buddhists. Translated by E. M. Hare, London: Geoffrey Cumberlege, Oxford University Press, 1947 [first published, 1945].

Thag. The Thera- and Therī-gāthā Part I, Theragāthā (PTS edition)

Psalms of the Early Buddhists I. — Psalms of the Sisters and *II. — Psalms of the Brethren.* Translated by Mrs. Rhys Davids, London: Luzac & Company, Ltd., 1964 [first published 1909 (Part I), 1913 (Part II)].

Ud. Udāna (PTS edition)

The Minor Anthologies of the Pali Canon Part II., Udāna: Verses of Uplift and Itivuttaka: As It Was Said. Translated by F. L. Woodward, London: Geoffrey Cumberlege, Oxford University Press, 1948 [first published in 1935].

V. The Vinaya Piṭakam (PTS edition)

The Book of the Discipline (Vinaya-Piṭaka). Vols. I-VI, translated by I. B. Horner, London: Published for the Pali Text Society by Luzac & Company, Ltd., 1949 (Vol. I), 1957 (Vols. II-III), 1962 (Vol. IV), 1963 (Vol. V), 1966 (Vol. VI) [Vols. I-V first published 1938-1952].

The correlations of the Pāli text (PTS edition) and *The Book of the Discipline* is as follows:

V. I, *The Book of the Discipline,* Vol. IV
V. II, *The Book of the Discipline,* Vol. V
V. III.1-194, *The Book of the Discipline,* Vol. I

V. III.195-IV.124, *The Book of the Discipline,* Vol. II
V. IV.124-end of IV, *The Book of the Discipline,* Vol. III
V. V, *The Book of the Discipline,* Vol. VI

Vism. Visuddhimagga (PTS edition)

The Path of Purification (Visuddhimagga) by Bhadantācariya Buddhaghosa. Translated by Bhikkhu Ñyāṇamoli, 2nd edition, Colombo: Published by A. Semage and printed at M. D. Gunasena & Co., Ltd., 1964.

Appendix II

Commentaries on the Pāli Canon

THE THERAVĀDA TRADITION possesses a rich and important commentarial literature which has been transmitted alongside the canon. According to the Theravāda, this commentarial literature provides the authoritative interpretation of the Pāli Canon, the *Tipiṭaka*. The Commentaries represent the Theravādin solution to a Buddhist hermeneutical problem of how ordinary people can understand correctly the profound teachings of the enlightened Buddha. Theravadins have vouchsafed the authority of the commentarial tradition by tracing its origins to the Buddha himself and to his great disciples who "explained the teachings given in brief."

From a critical standpoint one may question the attribution of the commentarial explanations to the Buddha or even to the earliest period of the Buddhist tradition since the strata of this commentarial literature gradually developed over time as the ongoing, oral commentarial tradition became fixed.[1] The shape of the commentarial literature points up both its central hermeneutical function and its successive waves of interpretation: each Pāli text has its Pāli *Aṭṭhakathā* or Commentary, each *Aṭṭhakathā* is explained by one or more *Tīkās* or Sub-Commentaries, and the *Ṭīkās* in turn are further commented upon by *Anuṭikās*, or Lesser Sub-Commentaries, with the whole process extending over almost two thousand years.

The central point to be grasped about this whole system of commentarial literature, however, is that it functions in the Theravāda tradition as the necessary, essential and authoritative interpretation of the canon. Thus, if one wants to know how Theravādins have traditionally understood the teachings of the Buddha (on, for example, the question of refuge), one must read the Pāli texts in the light of the commentaries.

1. See George D. Bond, *"The Word of the Buddha": The Tipiṭaka and Its Interpretation in Theravāda Buddhism*. (Forthcoming, M. D. Gunasena and Co., Colombo, Sri Lanka).

To assist the reader in approaching the commentarial tradition, we list below the Pāli *Aṭṭhakathās* or Commentaries, the first and most important stratum of the literature, arranged according to the texts of the *Tipiṭaka*.

Canonical Text	**Commentator**[2]	**Commentary**[3]
I. Vinaya Piṭaka	Buddhaghosa	*Samamtapāsādikā* Vols. I-VII. Ed. by J. Takakusa and M. Negai. London: Pali Text Society, 1924-27.
Pātimokkha	Buddhaghosa	*Kaṇkhāvitaraṇī*. Ed. D. A. L. Maskell. London: Pali Text Society, 1956.
II. Sutta Piṭaka		
Dīgha Nikāya	Buddhaghosa	*Sumaṇgalavilāsinī*, Vol. I. Ed. by T. W. Rhys Davids & Carpenter. London: P.T.S., 1886. Vols. II & III. Ed. by W. Stede. Portions translated into English in various publications, e.g., Bhikkhu Bodhi, *The Discourse on the All-Embracing Net of Views: The Brahmajāla Sutta and its Commentaries*. Kandy: Buddhist Publication Society, 1978.
Majjhima-Nikāya	Buddhaghosa	*Papañcasūdanī*, Vols, I & II. Ed. by J. H. Woods and D. Kosambi. London: P.T.S., 1922, 1928. Vol. III-V. Ed. by I. B. Horner. London: P.T.S., 1933-38. Portions translated into English, e.g., Ñyāṇaponika Thera, *The Threefold Refuge* (cited above under MA. in Appendix I). Another portion of this commentary has been translated in Soma Thera, *The Way of Mindfulness: The Satipaṭṭhāna Sutta and Commentary*. Kandy: Buddhist Publication Society, 1941.
Saṃyutta-Nikāya	Buddhaghosa	*Sāratthappakāsinī*, Vols. I-III. Ed. by F. L. Woodward. London: P.T.S., 1929-37.
Aṅguttara-Nikāya	Buddhaghosa	*Manorathapūraṇī*, Vols. I-II. Ed. by M. Walleser. London: P.T.S., 1924-30. Vols. III-V. Ed. by H. Kopp. London: P.T.S., 1936-57.

2. Under the category "Commentator" are listed the names of commentators who drew upon older commentaries and the older commentarial tradition to compile the Pāli commentaries. These commentators are not to be considered strictly as authors of the commentaries.

3. Those instances where English translations exist are indicated. Otherwise, the commentaries listed here are in the Roman script transliteration of the Pāli language as adopted by the Pali Text Society.

Canonical Text	Commentator	Commentary
Khuddaka-Nikāya		
1. *Khuddakapāṭha*	Buddhaghosa	*Paramatthajotikā* I. Ed. (together with *Khp.*), by H. Smith. London: P.T.S., 1915. Translation: *The Minor Readings (Khp.) and the Illustrator of Ultimate Meaning*, Part I. Bhikkhu Ñāṇamoli. London: P.T.S., 1960
2. *Dhammapada*	Buddhaghosa	*Dhammapada-Aṭṭhakathā*, Vol. I-IV. Ed. by H. C. Norman. London: P.T.S., 1909-14. Index ed. L. Tailang, 1915. Commentarial stories translated in E. W. Burlingame, *Buddhist Legends*, 3 vols., London: P.T.S., 1921. New translation of verses and commentarial glosses forthcoming by John Ross Carter and M. Palihawadana.
3. *Udāna*	Dhammapāla	*Paramatthadīpanī* I. Ed. by F. L. Woodward. London: P.T.S., 1926.
4. *Itivuttaka*	Dhammapāla	*Paramatthadīpanī* II, Vols. I-II. Ed. by M. M. Bose. London: P.T.S., 1934-36.
5. *Suttanipāta*	Buddhaghosa	*Paramatthajotikā* II, Vols. I-III. Ed. by H. Smith. London: P.T.S., 1916-18.
6. *Vimānavatthu*	Dhammapāla	*Paramatthadīpanī* III. Ed. by E. Hardy. London: P.T.S., 1901.
7. *Petavatthu*	Dhammapāla	*Paramatthadīpanī* IV. Ed. by E. Hardy. London: P.T.S., 1894.
8. *Theragāthā*	Dhammapāla	*Paramatthadīpanī* V, Vols. I-III. Ed. by F. L. Woodward. London: P.T.S., 1940-59. Partially translated along with the text in *Psalms of the Brethren*, trans. C. Rhys Davids, London: P.T.S. 1937
9. *Therīgāthā*	Dhammapāla	*Paramatthadīpanī* VI. Ed. by E. Muller. London: P.T.S., 1893. Partially translated along with text in *Psalms of the Sisters*, trans. C. Rhys Davids, London: P.T.S., 1909.
10. *Jātaka*	Buddhaghosa	*Jātakaṭṭhakathā* or *Jātakaatthavaṇṇanā*. Publ. as *The Jataka together with its Commentary*. Ed. by V. Fausboll. London: 1877-97. Translated as *Jātaka Stories*, trans. E. B. Cowell, London: P.T.S., 1895-1907.
11. *Niddesa*	Upasena	*Saddhammapajjotikā* Vols. I-III. Ed. by A. P. Buddhadatta. London: P.T.S., 1931-40.

Canonical Text	Commentator	Commentary
12. *Paṭisambhidāmagga*	Mahānāma	*Saddhammappakāsinī*, Vols. I-III. Ed. by C. V. Joshi. London: P.T.S., 1933-47.
13. *Apadāna*	Buddhaghosa	*Apadāna-Aṭṭhakathā*. Ed. by C. E. Godakumbura. London: P.T.S., 1954.
14. *Buddhavaṃsa*	Buddhadatta	*Madhuratthavilāsinī*. Ed. by I. B. Horner. London: P.T.S., 1946.
15. *Cariyāpiṭaka*	Dhammapāla	*Paramatthadīpanī* VII. Ed. by D. L. Barua. London: P.T.S., 1939.
III. *Abhidhamma Piṭaka*		
Dhammasaṇgaṇi	Buddhaghosa	*Atthasālinī*. Ed. by E. Muller. London: P.T.S., 1897. Translated as *The Expositor* Vols. I-II, trans. Pe Maung Tin. London: P.T.S., 1920-21.
Vibhaṅga	Buddhaghosa	*Sommoha-vinodanī*. Ed. by A. P. Buddhadatta. London: P.T.S., 1923.
Kathāvatthu	Buddhaghosa	*Kathāvatthuppakaraṇa-Aṭṭhakathā*. Ed. by Minayeff. London: P.T.S., 1889. Translated as *The Debates Commentary* by B. C. Law. London: P.T.S., 1940.
Puggalapaññatti	Buddhaghosa	*Puggalapaññatti Aṭṭhakathā*, Ed. by G. Landsberg & C. Rhys Davids. London: P.T.S. Journal, 1914.
Dhātukathā	Buddhaghosa	*Dhātukathāppakaraṇa-Aṭṭakathā*. Ed. together with text, by E. Ṛ. Gooneratne. London: P.T.S., 1892.
Yamaka	Buddhaghosa	*Yamaka Commentary*. Ed. by C. Rhys Davids. London: P.T.S. Journal, 1912.
Paṭṭhāna	Buddhaghosa	*Paṭṭhānappakaraṇa Aṭṭhakathā*.

Abbreviations

A.	*The Aṅguttara-nikāya* (PTS edition)
AA.	*Manorathapūraṇī*: the commentary on the *Aṅguttara-nikāya* (PTS edition)
BuA.	*Madhuratthavilāsinī nāma Buddhavaṃsaṭṭhakathā* (PTS edition)
D.	*The Dīgha-nikāya* (PTS edition)
DA.	*The Sumaṅgala-vilāsinī*: the commentary on the *Dīgha-nikāya* (PTS edition)
Dhp.	*The Dhammapada* (PTS edition)
DhpA.	*The Commentary on the Dhammapada: Dhammapadaṭṭhakathā* (PTS edition)
JāA.	*The Jātaka: Together with Its Commentary* (PTS edition)
KhpA.	*The Khuddaka-Pāṭha: Together with Its Commentary Paramatthajotikā I* (PTS edition)
M.	*Majjhima-nikāya* (PTS edition)
MA.	*Papañcasūdanī Majjhimanikāyaṭṭhakathā*: the commentary on the *Majjhima-nikāya* (PTS edition)
PTS	The Pali Text Society
S.	The *Saṃyutta-nikāya* (PTS edition)
SA.	*Sārattha-ppakāsinī*: the commentary on the *Saṃyutta-nikāya* (PTS edition)
Sdpj.	*Saddhamma-pajjotikā*: the commentary on the *Mahāniddesa* (PTS edition)
Sn.	*Sutta-Nipāta* (PTS edition)
SnA.	*Sutta-Nipāta Commentary: Being Paramatthajotikā II* (PTS edition)
Thag.	*The Thera- and Therī-gāthā* Part I, *Theragāthā* (PTS edition)
ThagA.	*Paramattha-Dīpanī Theragāthā-Aṭṭhakathā*: the commentary on the *Theragāthū* (PTS edition)
Ud.	*Udāna* (PTS edition)
V.	*The Vinaya Piṭakam* (PTS edition)
Vism.	*Visuddhimagga* (PTS edition)

Bibliography

Books, Articles, and Translations, in Western Languages, Occurring in Notes to Chapters I-IV

Arvon, Henry. *Buddhism.* Translated by Douglas Scott, New York: Walker and Co., 1964.

The Book of the Discipline. Vol. IV, translated by I. B. Horner, London: Luzac & Company Ltd., 1962.

Buddharakkhita, Bhikkhu V. "Devotion in Buddhism," *Devotion in Buddhism,* Wheel Publication No. 18, Kandy: Buddhist Publication Society, 1960.

Buddhism and Christianity: Being an Oral Debate at Panadura Between the Rev. Migettuvatte Gunananda & the Rev. David de Silva. Introduction and Annotations by J. M. Peebles, Colombo: Mahabodhi Press, n.d.

Burnouf, E. *Introduction à l'histoire du buddhisme indien.* Paris: Imprimerie Royale, 1844.

Carter, John Ross. "*Dhamma* as a Religious Concept: A Brief Investigation of Its History in the Western Academic Tradition and Its Centrality within the Sinhalese Theravāda Tradition," *Journal of the American Academy of Religion,* Vol. 44, No. 4 (December, 1976), pp. 661-674.

__________________. *Dhamma: Western Academic and Sinhalese Buddhist Interpretations — a study of a religious concept.* Tokyo: The Hokuseido Press, 1978.

Clough, B. *A Sinhalese-English Dictionary.* New and enlarged edition, Colombo: Wesleyan Mission Press, 1892.

The Collection of The Middle Length Sayings (Majjhima-nikāya). Vol. II, translated by I. B. Horner, London: Published for the Pali Text Society by Luzac & Company, Ltd., 1957.

Davids, Mrs. C. A. F. Rhys. *Buddhism: A Study of the Buddhist Norm.* London: William and Norgate, n.d. [1912].

____________________. *A Manual of Buddhism: For Advanced Students.* London: The Sheldon Press, 1932.

Dialogues of the Buddha. Part I, translated by T. W. Rhys Davids. London: Luzac & Company, Ltd., 1956.

Dialogues of the Buddha. Part II, translated by T. W. and C. A. F. Rhys Davids, 4th edition. London: Published for the Pali Text Society by Luzac & Company Ltd., 1959.

Edgerton, Franklin. "Dominant Ideas in the Formation of Indian Culture," *Journal of the American Oriental Society*, Vol. 62 (Sept. 1942).

Geiger, Magdalene und Wilhelm. *Pāli Dhamma: vornehmlich in der kanonischen Literatur*. "Abhandlungen der Bayerischen Akademie der Wissenschaften; Philosophisch-philologische und historiche Klasse," Band XXXI, 1. Abhandlung (vorgelegt am 1, Mai, 1920). München: Verlag der Bayerischen Akademie der Wissenschaften, 1920.

Gombrich, Richard. *Precept and Practice: Traditional Buddhism in the Rural Highlands of Ceylon*. Oxford: Clarendon Press, 1971.

Hardy, R. Spence. *Eastern Monachism: An Account of the Origin, Laws, Discipline, Sacred Writings, Mysterious Rites, Religious Ceremonies, and Present Circumstances of the Order of Mendicants founded by Gótama Budha.* London: Partridge and Oakey, 1850.

Humphreys, Christmas. *Buddhism*. Hammondsworth, Middlesex: Penguin Books, Ltd., 1958.

Keith, A. Berriedale. *Buddhist Philosophy in India and Ceylon*. Oxford: The Clarendon Press, 1923.

King, Winston L. *Buddhism and Christianity: Some Bridges of Understanding*. London: George Allen and Unwin Ltd., 1963.

________________. *In the Hope of Nibbāna*. Lasalle, Illinois: Open Court Publishing Co., 1964.

Malalgoda, Kitsiri. *Buddhism in Sinhalese Society 1750-1900: A Study of Religious Revival and Change*. Berkeley: University of California Press, 1976.

The Minor Readings and the Illustrator of Ultimate Meaning. Translated by Bhikkhu Ñānamoli, London: Luzac & Co., Ltd., 1960.

Narain, A. K., general editor. *Studies in Pali and Buddhism*. Delhi: B. R. Publishing Corporation, 1979.

Ñyāṇaponika Thera. *The Threefold Refuge*. "The Wheel Series," No. 76, Kandy, Ceylon: Buddhist Publication Society, 1965.

The Pali Text Society's Pali-English Dictionary. Edited by T. W. Rhys Davids and William Stede, London: Luzac & Co., Ltd., 1966.

The Path of Purification (Visuddhimagga) by Bhadantācariya Buddhaghosa. Translated by Bhikkhu Ñyāṇamoli, Colombo: M. D. Gunasena & Co., Ltd., 1964.

Perry, Edmund F., and Shanta Ratnayaka. "The Sangha of the Tiratana," *REI Occasional Papers*, No. 1. Evanston, Illinois: Published by Religion and Ethics Institute, Inc., 1974.

Piyadassi Thera. *The Buddha's Ancient Path*. London: Rider & Company, 1964.
Rahula, Walpola. *The Heritage of the Bhikkhu*. New York: Grove Press, 1974.
____________. *What the Buddha Taught*. Revised edition. Bedford, England: Gordon Fraser, 1967.
Saddhatissa, H. *Buddhist Ethics: Essence of Buddhism*. London: George Allen & Unwin Ltd., 1970.
Slater, Robert Lawson. *Paradox and Nirvana: a study of religious ultimates with special reference to Burmese Buddhism*. Chicago, Illinois: The University of Chicago Press, 1951.
Smith, Wilfred Cantwell. *Faith and Belief*. Princeton: Princeton University Press, 1979.
____________. "Religious Atheism: Early Buddhist and Recent American," *Milla wa-Milla*, No. 6 (December, 1966), pp. 5-30.
Swearer, Donald K. 'The Appeal of Buddhism: A Christian Perspective," *The Christian Century*, November 3, 1971).
Weber, Max. *The Religion of India: The Sociology of Hinduism and Buddhism*. Translated and edited by H. Gerth and D. Martindale. New York: The Free Press, 1958.

Pāli and Sinhalese Sources Occurring in Notes to Chapters I-IV

The Aṅguttara-nikāya. Part I, edited by the Rev. Richard Morris, 2nd ed., revised by A. K. Warder, London: Published for the Pali Text Society by Luzac & Co., Ltd., 1961.
The Aṅguttara-nikāya. Part II, edited by the Rev.Richard Morris, London: Published for the Pali Text Society by Luzac & Co., Ltd., 1955.
Candavimala, Rērukānē. *Pohoya Dinaya*. Colombo: A. D. P. Sugatadāsa, Anula Mudraṇālaya, 1966.
____________. *Sūvisi Maha Guṇaya*. Colombo: A. D. P. Sugatadāsa, Anula Mudraṇālaya, 1969.
The Commentary on the Dhammapada. Vol. III, edited by H. C. Norman, London: Published for the Pali Text Society by Henry Frowde, Oxford University Press, 1912.
The Dhammapada. New edition by Sūriyagoḍa Sumaṅgala Thera, London: Published for the Pali Text Society by Humphrey Milford, 1914.
Dhammapāla's Paramattha-Dīpanī. Part IV, Being the Commentary on the *Vimāna-Vatthu*, edited by E. Hardy, London: Published for the Pali Text Society by Henry Frowde, Oxford University Press, 1901.
Dharmapradīpikā. Edited by Baddēgama Vimalavaṃsa Thera, 2nd ed., Colombo: M. D.Guṇasēna & Co., 1967.

The Dīgha Nikāya. Vol. II, edited by T. W. Rhys Davids and J. Estlin Carpenter, The Pali Text Society, London: Geoffrey Cumberlege, Oxford University Press, 1947.

Jātaka Aṭuvā Gäṭapadaya. Edited by Mäda-Uyangoḍa Vimalakīrti Thera and Nāhinnē Sominda Thera, Colombo: M.D. Guṇasēna & Co., 1961.

The Jātaka: Together with Its Commentary. Vols. I-VI, edited by V. Fausbøll, London: Published for the Pali Text Society by Messrs. Luzac & Co., Ltd., 1962 (Vol. I), 1963 (Vols. II-V), 1964 (Vol.V).

The Khuddaka-Pāṭha: Together with Its Commentary Paramatthajotikā I. Edited by Helmer Smith from a collation by Mabel Hunt, London: Published for the Pali Text Society by Luzac & Co., Ltd., 1959.

Madhuratthavilāsinī nāma Buddhavaṃsaṭṭhakathā of Bhadantācariya Buddhadatta Mahāthera. Edited by I. B. Horner, London: Published for the Pali Text Society by Humphrey Milford, Oxford University Press, 1946.

Majjhima-nikāya. Vol. I, edited by V. Trenckner, Vol. II-III, edited by Robert Chalmers, London: Published for the Pali Text Society by Luzac & Co., 1964 (Vol. I), 1960 (Vol. II-III).

Manorathapūraṇī: Buddhaghosa's Commentary on the Aṅguttaranikāya. Vol. II, edited by Max Walleser ahd Herman Kopp, London: Published for the Pali Text Society by the Oxford University Press, 1930.

Niddesa I: Mahāniddesa. Edited by L. de La Vallée Poussin and E. J. Thomas, London: Published for the Pali Text Society by Humphrey Milford, Oxford University Press, 1916 (Vol. I), 1917 (Vol. II).

Papañcasūdanī Majjhimanikāyaṭṭhakathā of Buddhaghosācariya. Parts I-II, edited by J. H. Woods and D. Kosambi, London: Published for the Pali Text Society by the Oxford University Press, 1922 (Part I), 1923 (Part II).

Paramattha-Dīpanī Theragāthā-Aṭṭhakathā: The Commentary of Dhammapālācariya. Vols. II-III, edited by F. L. Woodward, London: Published for the Pali Text Society by Messrs. Luzac & Co., Ltd., 1952 (Vol. II), 1959 (Vol. III).

Paramattha-Dīpanī Udānaṭṭhakathā (Udāna Commentary) of Dhammapālācariya. Edited by F. L. Woodward, London: Published for the Pali Text Society by the Oxford University Press, 1926.

Pānadurē Vādaya. Edited by P. A. Peiris and James Dias, Colombo: Laṅka Free Press, n.d.

Paramatthamañjūsā of Bhadantācariya Dhammapāla Thera: Or The Commentary of the Visuddhimagga. Vols. I-III, edited by Morontuḍuwē Dhammānanda Thera, Colombo: Mahabodhi Press, 1928 (Vol. I), 1930 (Vol. II), 1949 (Vol. III).

Saddhamma-pajjotikā: The Commentary on the Mahā-Niddesa. Vols. I-II, edited by A. P. Buddhadatta, London: Published for the Pali Text Society by Humphrey Milford, Oxford University Press, 1931 (Vol. I), 1939 (Vol. II).

Saddharmālaṅkāraya. Edited by Kiriällē Ñāṇavimala Thera, Colombo: M.D. Guṇasēna, 1954.

Saddharmaratnākaraya. Edited by Kaḷupaluvāvē Devānanda Thera, Colombo: Ratnākara Pot Veḷaṅda Śālāva, 1955.

Saddharmaratnāvaliya. Edited by Kiriällē Ñāṇavimala Thera, Colombo: M.D. Guṇasēna, 1961.

Saddharma Sārārtha Sangrahaya. Edited by Kiriällē Ñāṇavimala Thera, Colombo: M. D. Guṇasēna, 1957.

Saṃyutta-nikāya. Parts I-V, edited by M. Léon Feer, London: Published for the Pali Text Society by Messrs. Luzac & Co., Ltd., 1960.

Sārattha-ppakāsinī: Buddhaghosa's Commentary on the Saṃyutta-nikāya. Vols. I-III, edited by F. L.Woodward, London: Published for the Pali Text Society by Humphrey Milford, Oxford University Press, 1929 (Vol. I), 1932 (Vol. II), 1937 (Vol. III).

Somissara, Māpalagama Siri. *Buddha Dharma Mārgaya.* Colombo: Vijayasēna saha Sahōdarayo, 1967.

Śrī Saddharmāvavāda Saṃgrahaya. Edited by Vēragoḍa Amaramoli Thera, Colombo: Ratnākara Mudraṇālayaya, 1956.

Sumaṅgala-vilāsinī: Buddhaghosa's Commentary on the Dīgha-Nikāya. Part I, edited by T. W. Rhys Davids and J. Estlin Carpenter, London: Published for the Pali Text Society by Henry Frowde, Oxford University Press, 1886.

Sutta-Nipāta. New edition by Dines Andersen and Helmer Smith, London: Published for the Pali Text Society by Geoffrey Cumberlege, Oxford University Press, 1948.

Sutta-Nipāta Commentary: Being Paramatthajotikā II. Vols. I-II, edited by Helmer Smith, London: Published for the Pali Text Society by Humphrey Milford, Oxford University Press, 1916 (Vol. I), 1917 (Vol. II).

The Thera- and Therī-gāthā: (Stanzas Ascribed to Elders of the Buddhist Order of Recluses). Edited by Hermann Oldenberg and Richard Pischel, 2nd ed., with Appendices by K.R. Norman and L. Alsdorf, London: Published for the Pali Text Society, Luzac & Co., Ltd., 1966.

Udāna. Edited by Paul Steinthal, London: Published for the Pali Text Society by Geoffrey Cumberlege, Oxford University Press, 1948.

Upāsakajanālaṅkāra. Edited by H. Saddhatissa, London: Published for the Pali Text Society, Luzac & Co., Ltd., 1965.

Vaṃsatthappakāsini: Commentary on the Mahāvaṃsa. Vols. I-II, edited by G. P. Malalasekera for the Government of Ceylon,

London: Published for the Pali Text Society by Humphrey Milford, Oxford University Press, 1935.

The Vimāna-Vatthu: of the Khuddaka Nikāya Sutta Piṭaka. Edited by Edmund Rowland Gooneratne, London: Published for the Pali Text Society by Henry Froude [sic], Oxford University Press, n.d. [1886?].

The Vinaya Piṭakam. Vols. I-V, edited by Hermann Oldenberg, London: Published for the Pali Text Society, Luzac & Co., Ltd., 1964.

The Visuddhi-magga of Buddhaghosa. Vol. I, edited by C. A. F. Rhys Davids, London: Published for the Pali Text Society by Humphrey Milford, Oxford University Press, 1920.

List of Authors

George Doherty Bond is Associate Professor of the History and Literature of Religions at Northwestern University. He received his B.A. degree from Texas Tech University, his B.D. from Southern Methodist University, and his Ph.D. degree from Northwestern University. A recipient of a Fulbright-Hays grant, he conducted research in Sri Lanka, 1970-1971, and has returned again to carry out his studies. He has served on the faculties of Purdue University and the University of Georgia.

Professor Bond is the author of *The Word of the Buddha: The Tipiṭaka and Its Interpretation in Theravāda Buddhism* (forthcoming from M. D. Gunasena and Co., Ltd., Colombo, Sri Lanka). Among his published essays are "The *Netti-Pakaraṇa:* A Theravāda Method of Interpretation" in *Buddhist Studies in Honor of Walpola Rahula* (London: Gordon Fraser, 1980), and "Theravāda Buddhism's Meditations on Death and the Symbolism of Initiatory Death," *History of Religions,* Vol. 19, No. 3 (February, 1980).

John Ross Carter is Associate Professor of Philosophy and Religion, and Director of Chapel House at Colgate University. He received his B.A. degree from Baylor University, his B.D. from the Southern Baptist Theological Seminary, his M.Th. degree, in an intercollegiate program with King's College and the School of Oriental and African Studies, from the University of London, and his Ph.D. degree from Harvard University. A recipient of a Fulbright-Hays grant, he conducted research in Sri Lanka, 1968-1971, and has returned frequently to continue his studies.

Professor Carter is the author of *Dhamma: Western Academic and Sinhalese Buddhist Interpretations — a study of a religious concept* (Tokyo: The Hokuseido Press, 1978), and the editor of *Religiousness in Sri Lanka* (Colombo: Marga Institute, 1979). Among his published essays are "A History of *Early Buddhism,*" *Religious Studies,* Vol. 13, No. 3 (September, 1977), and "Translational Theology: An Expression of Christian Faith in a Religiously Plural World," in *Christian Faith in a Religiously Plural World,* edited by D. G. Dawe and John B. Carman (Maryknoll, New York: Orbis Books, 1978).

Edmund F. Perry is Professor of the Comparative Study of Religion and longtime chairman of the Department of the History and Literature of Religions at Northwestern University. He received his A.B. from the University of Georgia, his B.D. from Candler School of Theology, Emory University, his Ph.D. from Northwestern University, and a D.Litt. from Vidyodaya University of Sri Lanka.

Professor Perry, who taught at Vidyodaya University in Sri Lanka on a Fulbright-Hays Professorship (1967-1968), most recently has co-edited *Buddhist Studies in Honour of Walpola Rahula* (London: Gordon Fraser, 1980) a volume presented to the Venerable Rahula in a national ceremony organized and presided over by President J. R. Jayewardene of the Democratic Socialist Republic of Sri Lanka.

Shanta Ratnayaka is Associate Professor of Philosophy and Religion at the University of Georgia. He received his B.A. degree with First Class Honors from Vidyodaya University in Sri Lanka. A recipient of a Fulbright-Hays grant for graduate studies, 1969-1972, he received his M.A. and his Ph.D. degrees from Northwestern University.

Professor Ratnayaka is the author of *Two Ways of Perfection: Buddhist and Christian* (Colombo: Lake House Investments Ltd., 1978), and a forthcoming monograph in Sinhalese, *Buddhism: Its History, Doctrine, Ethics, and Culture* (Colombo: M. D. Gunasena and Co., Ltd.). Among his published essays are "The Religious Interpretation of Nirvāna," *Insight: A Journal of World Religions*, Vol. 1, No. 1, 1976, and "A Buddhist – Christian Monastic Dialogue," *Dialogue* (Colombo), New Series, Vol. 6, No. 3, 1979.

Index